C000297939

AN ODE
TO DARKNESS

AN ODE TO DARKNESS

SIGRI SANDBERG

Translated by Siân Mackie

SPHERE

First published in Great Britain in 2019 by Sphere

1 3 5 7 9 10 8 6 4 2

A CIP catalogue record for this book
is available from the British Library.

ISBN 978-0-7515-7864-5

Typeset in Garamond by M Rules
Printed and bound in Great Britain by
Clays Ltd, Elcograf S.p.A.

Papers used by Sphere are from well-managed forests
and other responsible sources.

Sphere
An imprint of
Little, Brown Book Group
Carmelite House
50 Victoria Embankment
London EC4Y 0DZ

An Hachette UK Company
www.hachette.co.uk

www.littlebrown.co.uk

For Vinjar, Styrk and Steinar

Contents

Contents

You can never see further than in the dark.

JON FOSSE

Prologue

When did you last see the stars?

Look at a satellite image of the Earth. Where it was once as dark as night, it is now lit up like a Christmas tree. If you zoom in on a city, you'll see floodlights, neon lights, car lights and street lights. If you zoom in even further, to your own bedroom, you might see lamps and television, tablet and phone screens.

If you live in a city and look out of the window, there will be a greyish-yellow haze between you and the Milky Way. Even if it is night. Even if it is winter.

Humans have always struggled with the dark, but isn't it light enough now? What is all this artificial light doing to us and everything else that lives? What is it doing to our sleep patterns and rhythms and bodies?

I live in Norway, the land of the polar night. I have a cabin in the mountains in Finse, 195 kilometres north-west of Oslo. Darkness and stars can still be experienced there, particularly now during the darkest months of the year. I pack my bag and head up there. To seek out natural darkness, knowledge and the night sky – and to see how long I dare stay.

Because paradoxically, I am afraid of the dark, and that fear is all-consuming, at least when I'm completely alone.

There aren't any roads to Finse, so I buy a train ticket.

DAY 1

Monday

The train rattles out of the city. It's early on Monday morning. The city twinkles and flashes, still awash in artificial light. I leave my big blue backpack with the suitcases and bags at the end of Coach 4 before finding my seat, number 36.

I spend most of my time here in Oslo in a tower block with a view of the city. I can see all the way to the fjord, across several thousand rooftops, and I can see a bit of forest. But at night, everything is transformed into crackling, luminous noise. A steady hum occasionally interrupted by other, more abrupt sounds. All big cities are bathed in artificial light at night. The light from Oslo reaches 150 to 200 kilometres out of the city in every direction. This makes it difficult to see the night sky properly here – and impossible to see the Milky Way.

3

The train rattles onwards, and it soon starts getting lighter outside. Coach 4 buzzes with conversation and movement, low music, people slurping coffee and a conductor, smart in a hat, coughing and checking tickets. I've brought my laptop and several books. One of them is about a woman who, in 1934, was on her way out of another city. Christiane Ritter was travelling to the far north, all the way to Svalbard, an archipelago located midway between mainland Norway and the North Pole. To a darkness and a winter she knew nothing about. Wondering how dark it would get that close to the Pole and how she would cope.

Christiane

Christiane was an upper-class woman from Bohemia, which at that time was part of Czechoslovakia. Her husband, Hermann Ritter, was a trapper in Svalbard. He tried to tempt her north to Gråhuken in Spitsbergen, the largest island in the archipelago. She did not really want to go – she was enjoying painting and spending time with her four-year-old daughter and friends – but her husband wrote one, two, three letters saying: 'Leave everything as it is and follow me to the Arctic.'

He wrote that it would be impossible for him to describe everything. The endless light in the summer. The long darkness in the winter. She would have to come and experience it for herself. She eventually let herself be convinced, packing a bag and beginning her journey in the summer of 1934. She brought along a Bible, camel-hair underwear, dried parsley and painting supplies. She boarded a boat that took her further and further north, up the coast of Norway. Past landscape that was increasingly barren and desolate.

She passes the northernmost point of the mainland and continues on past Bear Island, but when the other passengers find out where she is going, they are horrified. 'Oh, now, you mustn't go there. You'll freeze to death on that island. It's no place for you, little lady. Besides, you might get scurvy.'

She is met by her husband on the north-west coast of Spitsbergen, in Ny-Ålesund, from where they plan to travel onwards in a smaller boat. Many of the people there are well acquainted with the archipelago. They talk about it loudly and at length, with one Norwegian claiming that spring is the best time of year. Christiane doubts that she will come to share this view, stubbornly opining that she will never be as taken with the landscape as they are. 'Oh, you will be,' the Norwegian says, quietly but assuredly.

Christiane's first glimpse of Gråhuken is as a forlorn, grey, elongated strip of coast off in the distance. She can also see the cabin, a tiny box that is almost indistinguishable from the landscape. So this is where she is to stay. With her husband – and one other trapper. For one year. For one long, wild winter. No one on the boat speaks apart from an elderly man, who says a few words to her in German. 'My gracious lady, you simply cannot spend the winter here. It would be quite foolish!'

Everything is grey and rainy. Christiane thinks it is a gruesome place. 'Nothing but water, fog and rain. It presses in on the people here until they lose their minds. What business would anyone have on such an island? How much hope, how many noble plans have been reduced to nothing here, how many enterprises have ended in shipwreck, and not least: how many human lives have been claimed by this landscape?'

They take their luggage ashore and she explores the tiny trapper's cabin. It measures 7.42 by 1.28 metres, covering an area of less than 10 square metres. And it is located 250 kilometres from the nearest city, Longyearbyen. When the boat leaves, there is no knowing when they will next see other people. Satellite phones are yet to be developed, and no one will be able to rescue them if anything happens.

The stove doesn't work at all, and the fog hangs thick around them. Christiane turns to her husband. 'Where is the boudoir that you promised me in your letters?' she asks.

It is August, summertime, always light outside. Always grey outside.

Finse, 1,222 metres above sea level

I was born in August, and I like that time of the year. I like long, sunlit evenings when the fjord is warm. It's not surprising, really, since we humans are designed for warmer climes where there's no need for down jackets and woollen underwear. Since pre-historic times, our genes have been programmed to understand that it is light during the day and then that light wanes until it is dark at night.

Despite this, I've spent eight years living in Svalbard and I visit Finse a lot. I've zipped myself into my coat, put on my ski goggles and struggled through the wind and darkness for over forty years. And it feels as if snow and storms and slush, as if all of this has also become part of me. As if I need to get up there sometimes.

Finse is also the best place I know to see the stars.

But I'm not often there alone. I don't like being alone, not for prolonged periods of time, in any case. A few hours is fine. I mean, I've slept outdoors a few times, in the mountains and in snow caves and in tents when it's been -40 degrees – but always with another person there. With a man, with the kids, with friends. I don't like it, but I need to do it: to be alone in the mountains when it gets dark. I need to practise, because I like it there. I've moved around a lot in my life, but I keep coming back to Finse. This place and the cabin are constants for me, so I need to be able to be there without someone to hold me when darkness falls.

I need to be able to sit and write there, because I'm a journalist and I write reports and books, about nature and the North and people – and about how everything is connected in this unstable world. So maybe this trip is part of a bigger project, or maybe it's not. Maybe it's just stupid. Maybe I'll get to the cabin door and change my mind.

I look out of the train window at everything flying past. Trees become fewer and further between, finally disappearing altogether. I think about the kids and about my husband back in the city – I already miss them. I get off the train after four and a half hours. At Finse station, 1,222 metres above sea level, the highest railway station in Northern Europe.

Finse is referred to as the southernmost Arctic because, even though it is located south of the Arctic Circle and polar night does not occur here, the temperatures and landscapes are similar. There are no trees here. The average temperature throughout the year is below zero. All the old heroes came here. Ernest Shackleton came here to train for long and difficult polar expeditions. As did Fridtjof Nansen. There are also pictures of both the lake, Finsevatnet, and the glacier, Hardangerjøkulen, hanging in Roald Amundsen's house. The history of the place is all quite recent, as is the case for Svalbard. Finse only became a small community when the Bergen Line, which opened in 1909, was built.

Labourers migrated up from the lowlands, looking for work, and lived in small barracks in the mountains while they helped build the 492-kilometre railway line stretching from east to west. Deep in the darkest mountains they drilled and blasted tunnels using dynamite and their bare hands. The project pushed the limits of what was possible when it came to knowledge and technology at that time, and it was hard work. In the dust and the dirt and the dark, in snow and storms and pissing rain.

The Bergen Line was a bold, demanding and magnificent project – and cost the entire state budget at that time: 52.5 million Norwegian kroner. King Haakon referred to it as 'our generation's masterpiece' when he opened the line in November 1909. It was now possible to travel between Oslo and Bergen in fifteen hours. And to get off the train in the mountains. To stay in a nice hotel.

I'm the only person leaving the train in Finse today. There's still a nice hotel near the railway station. There's also a large tourist cabin a few hundred metres away. Everything is closed. It's low season. It's windy.

I fire up the stove and dread what is to come

I put on my skis and ski goggles and head towards the cabin. I pull my sled along behind me. It is laden with my backpack full of food and everything else I need to spend a few days here alone. As mentioned, there is no road leading to Finse, and the closest shop is miles away. I go no more than 3 kilometres through fresh snow, white landscape and wind, spot the cabin in the distance. Slide the key into the lock.

I unpack. The cabin is cold and I fire up the stove. I look out at the plateau and frozen lake and wind. It is almost three o'clock. It will start to get dark in an hour or so. The cabin is bigger and better than Christiane Ritter's – about five times as big. The stove is better, too: it even has glass doors so I can see the flames. They emit a nice yellow light.

I'm not sure whether I regret coming here. Well, I'm actually pretty sure I do. Even though I'm doing this of my own free will, I'm dreading the darkness so much that I can feel it in my chest and down in my feet. It hurts. I know the darkness will envelop me, not gently, but hard. I know the big windowpanes will turn black, that the landscape will disappear, and I know I'll feel heavier then. I can feel it in my bones, and I know me.

I make it a ritual straight away, from the very first evening. Sitting and letting it come. Letting my body relax, sitting there from dusk, crocheting, looking out, letting the blue hour embrace me. Not lighting or switching anything on to provide more light than what the stove gives, because then it will just be even blacker outside. Maybe I'm trying to bid the darkness welcome so it will be kinder to me.

I know that the worst will come when I eventually close my eyes to sleep. When I need to relinquish all control. I'm not afraid of wolves or ghosts or polar bears. So what am I afraid of?

I want to tell you about the dark.

I've been afraid of the dark since I was a little girl, a big sister who was often responsible for a throng of younger siblings.

'Remember to lock both doors,' I reminded my parents after one of them had sung me a goodnight song. I reminded them to lock the doors every night.

So no one would come in. In from the dark.

The word *darkness* and the cultural dichotomy

The word *darkness* gives me a kind of jolt. A hard jolt deep inside. It has connotations of grief and illness and night and the colour black – and my own fear of the dark.

Darkness is generally a negative word, a word that is heavy

11

and sad and pulls other words down with it. Dark heart. Dark days. Dark past. Dark path. Dark mood. Dark humour. Dark age. A dark chapter in our lives, in history. There often has to be light for everything to be well, in poems and songs and literature and life in general. As a child, I often left the hall light on and my door ajar.

Humankind has always struggled with both metaphorical and literal darkness. Darkness was an enemy, like the cold, something unsafe – and light was by definition good. In Greek mythology, it is said that fire was stolen from the gods. That after other animals were given all the best qualities, the Titan Prometheus stole fire and gave it to mankind as consolation. The king of the gods, Zeus, was furious and created woman to punish mankind.

Since then, people have sought more light. In the West, light is associated with truth, knowledge and being able to see. Light represents life and what is good; darkness, death and what is evil. In religious texts dating back thousands of years before Christ we find sun gods – and a dark and cold kingdom of the dead. The dichotomy of the light heaven and the dark hell has persisted in both subculture and popular culture. Light is safety; darkness loses its power in the light – and trolls turn to stone and shatter.

Has this cultural dichotomy prevented us from seeing that darkness can also be kind? Because it is only now, in the most recent seconds of human history, that someone has suggested that, ahem, darkness might also be important. Just a bit. For quite a lot of things.

I was born in 1975, so my generation and the one before grew up in and with electric light. It has not been properly dark anywhere other than far outside of towns and villages in my lifetime. Maybe that's why I'm afraid of the dark. Maybe that's why I haven't considered what we're in the process of losing.

In any case, let me try to define it more scientifically and specifically:

What is darkness?

When the sun is more than 18 degrees below the horizon, we achieve *astronomical darkness*. But because of the light pollution in the world, you need to venture far out on to the plateaus, into the desert or on to the open sea to really experience it. At the end of June, the American research base at the South Pole is perhaps the darkest place in the world inhabited by humans. Theoretically. If they switched off all the lights. And there wasn't any snow. Or stars.

13

To understand darkness, we also need to know something about light. Astrophysics defines darkness as an *absence of light*. In space, the distance between objects can be incomprehensibly vast, so when there is almost no distribution of light between what is shining and us, physicists say that darkness is the *absence of light in the direction we are looking*.

Darkness can therefore also be defined as a *perceived absence of light*.

This is actually true: very small quantities of light penetrate everywhere throughout the entire universe – it is just that our eyes cannot see it because they are too poorly designed. Humans can see light, which is made up of electromagnetic waves, when the distance between the waves is between 400 and 700 nanometres (a billionth of a metre). Warm, yellowish-red light has a greater distance between the waves and a lower frequency than cold, bluish-white light.

But the light that is visible to humans is not the only light in the universe. Radio waves, microwaves, infrared and ultraviolet radiation, X-rays and gamma rays are also energy – are also light. Some of these rays are reflected by the atmosphere; others find their way through.

The biggest problem with our eyes is that our pupils are so small, making it difficult for much light to enter at any given moment. Of course, we have found ways of enhancing our poor vision. Both cameras and telescopes are optical instruments with larger apertures than our eyes, and so, using mirrors and various devices, the light is gathered and adapted to allow us to see more than we can unaided, and far, far out into space – if it is dark enough.

It is a fundamental truth that darkness does not exist from an astronomical standpoint. Happy fact. I'm willing to accept this. I try to find it comforting, helpful. But I still struggle to completely believe that darkness does not actually exist. Because what does it matter to a small, poorly designed human whether darkness is real or perceived? And what about the black holes in the universe, what about dark matter, what about the night sky and the threats against it, and ... and now I'm exhausted. I'm done for the day. I feel so small, and I'm tired of being afraid.

I walk over to the window looking west, where the phone signal is best, and call my husband. Tell him I'm afraid. He says there isn't anything to be afraid of. I tell him that isn't much of a comfort.

I ask him to sing me a goodnight song. He sings.

Christiane

Christiane Ritter is a respectable lady. She is still wearing her hat and coat up in Gråhuken even though evenings are light in the kingdom of the midnight sun. In her first evening in the tiny cabin, she admits that she has no idea how to get into a sleeping bag.

'I am divested of my hat and coat, and then simply lifted up into the sleeping bag and rolled against the wall like a roulade.' And it is light all through the night. Or grey. Because the only thing she can see is fog. And rock. 'Rock upon rock, I see rock in my waking hours and in my sleep. I can tell it is going to get on my nerves. This rocky country with its vast, utter barrenness will haunt me like a bad dream.'

The cabin she lives in was built by legendary trapper Hilmar Nøis and his men in 1928. That autumn, Christiane's husband and his trapper friend Karl Nikolaisen build her a drift timber extension of a couple of square metres – the boudoir Hermann promised her.

Northerner Karl does not expect this to end well. He is convinced that the city lady from the far south will go mad if she has to spend much time alone. Pushed over the edge by the darkness, by the storms, by the men, by this tiny cabin.

Finally, the fog lifts. The men are often out trapping, tending to fox snares, shooting grouse. It is important that they find as much food as possible before the polar night draws in. Against all expectations, Christiane falls in love with the open land-scape, with the glaciers flowing into the sea, with the silence, with the fresh snow blanketing everything. The trapper's hut is called Kapp Hvile. 'The Cape of Repose'. It is one of the most beautiful names for a trapper's cabin that I have ever heard. Or rather, it *is* the most beautiful. Kapp Hvile.

Eventually autumn and darkness come to Gråhuken as well.

The polar night and a miner

When the sun doesn't rise or set, instead crossing the sky beneath the horizon, this is called polar night. This means you are located north of the Arctic Circle. Or south of the Antarctic Circle. These circles of latitude are abstract and not entirely static lines around the globe, running parallel to the Equator.

In a way, the polar night also extends down into Norway due to the high mountains and narrow valleys. To Rjukan in Telemark, for example, which sees no sunlight in the middle of winter. When Rjukan became an industrial town, a cable car was built up the mountainside so the workers could get some light during the Christmas period. They now have a lot of artificial light – and sun mirrors in the town centre. Those living on farms on the shores of the innermost part of Sognefjord, along Lustrafjord and in the village of Kroken have to make do without sunlight for eight whole weeks around Christmastime.

In Svalbard, it is pitch-black in the middle of winter. There isn't even any twilight. No blue hour. No grey. It's just as dark in the middle of the day as in the middle of the night. There, the sun is more than 6 degrees below the horizon, even in the middle of the day. This is called polar night. In Longyearbyen, this night lasts for around eight weeks.

During my first winter up there I was just fascinated. The town was illuminated, of course, but the darkness surrounding it was surreal.

In such a place, during such a long period of darkness, some artificial light is necessary. For well-being and safety, and to make sure things get done.

My first winter in the north was fun. My second, too. During my third I bought a daylight lamp to keep me awake so I could get some work done. In the end, during the sixth, seventh and eighth winters, it stopped being fun. I slept and slept.

Svein Jonny Albrigtsen is a miner, and I once interviewed him up there during the polar night. He has lived in Svalbard since 1974, since before I was born, and has worked in the mines for over thirty years. In recent years, he has caught the bus out of Longyearbyen to Mine 7, which is more than 10 kilometres outside town, inside a mountain, at 06:15 every morning. He doesn't see any light at all, not even when it starts getting lighter in February. He told me he feels more tired when it's dark everywhere, but that the polar night used to be darker, when there wasn't as much artificial light or as many street lights. When there weren't any planes. Back then, the last boat left in October and they were on their own all winter. Back then, he knew everyone in town, which is no longer the case.

But he's never been scared.

'I'm fine as long as my headlamp works,' he said.

Albrigtsen told me that others had struggled. That they hadn't been able to sleep when there was no difference between day and night.

And there are a lot of stories like that, about people not being able to cope with the endless darkness. People who were supposed to start work at 08:00, but didn't arrive until 14:00, then until 16:00, and weren't able to sleep until next morning, and everything was a mess. They moved south again quite quickly, the people who couldn't get to grips with the darkness.

I remember encountering some tourists who had made a spontaneous trip from Oslo to Svalbard one December. They ended up in the pub on a Friday night and were discussing what they would do the next day when it was light. They didn't believe us when we told them it wouldn't get light. They just laughed and laughed.

Finse station illuminated

Night is drawing in here in Finse. I can see it, feel it. I go outside behind the cabin to pee. That's what we do here. I don't take a headlamp. They have their uses, but the light they provide is somewhat limited, and the more you look at what is illuminated, the less you see of everything else, of the landscape, of the sky. Headlamps have become a lot brighter in recent years. If you encounter people wearing them while skiing, for example, your vision can be very impaired for a long time afterwards.

I pause, waiting for my eyes to adjust to the darkness – like a cat. Humans are among the animals with the poorest night vision. Cats have a field of vision of 285 degrees and see very well in the dark. However, it is a myth that they can see in total darkness. Instead, they use their other senses and get around using sounds, smells and their sensitive whiskers.

I can't see Finse station from here, but I'm pretty sure the clouds over the mountain behind the cabin are a bit yellower than the rest of the sky. Even though the hotel and tourist cabin are closed, and the station recently became unmanned despite major protests, they still emit some light, twenty-four hours a day, all year long.

Apart from that, I can't see much, despite the snow. I can just about make out the mountains. I can't see the rocks that well any more. The sky is dark clouds. Not a star in sight, no moon, nothing in particular. When I'm back inside, I pull a blanket around me. Feed another log to the stove. Look out the window. But then I change my mind. Best to look inwards now, into the fire.

Fear of the dark and the body's reaction

Our genetic material is ancient, designed to help us when we're in danger. In days gone by, it made sense to fear things like the dark, dizzying heights and poisonous spiders. On the whole, a healthy respect for the night was quite practical. For example, fear of the dark could prevent cave-dwellers from wandering around at night when they were vulnerable to attack and other dangers. It was better to sit by the fire, relax, sleep. Because when our vision is compromised, we lose control and perspective; our body tells us we need to be on guard, and our other senses, such as our senses of hearing and smell, become sharper.

This fear is no longer as crucial to our survival, but it has been given a name. Fear of or in the dark is called *achluophobia*. If it interferes with your day-to-day life, it is a phobia. And a phobia is an irrational, intense and persistent fear of particular situations, activities, objects, animals or people.

Professor of psychology Asle Hoffart says that achluophobia is *an exaggerated fear of being in the dark*.

21

'In the dark, you lose the perspective you have in the light. People with this phobia feel powerless and vulnerable. And if you also start thinking about dangerous things that might happen, this fear intensifies,' he says.

When we are afraid, this fear is processed by our amygdala. The amygdala is a structure in the brain that activates the sympathetic nervous system. This is part of the autonomic nervous system, over which we have no control. It is activated when we are in danger, putting us on high alert so that we are ready to deal with crises and hazards and God knows what.

It is in these situations that the hormone adrenaline is secreted into the blood. Here, it initiates a number of reactions: we breathe more rapidly, our hearts beat faster, we sweat and the blood flow to our muscles increases. Our bodies ready themselves to run or fight. Sometimes we even engage in catastrophic thinking.

Professor Hoffart likes the dark. He likes how it makes his thoughts, imagination and feelings – and physical sensations – clearer. He also delights in how uncertain and frightening the dark is.

But he has also made a list of tips for those with this phobia. These involve exposing yourself to what you're afraid of. Setting yourself a target, such as going to the outhouse on your own or walking along a dark path. You could always ask a friend to accompany you at first. And if you feel scared, Hoffart urges you to stand your ground, to take stock of your thoughts and feelings. Possibly even to step things up a notch and compound your fear. Step out of your comfort zone. Who knows, you might even find that the dark is actually quite nice and exciting.

It suddenly occurs to me that that's exactly what I'm doing. Exposing myself to the dark. Sitting here and letting it envelop me. Just *being* in the dark. But I'm not finding it nice or exciting. Not at all. I gaze into the flames as if they might possess some sort of power to help me.

Fire, milky seas and let it go

The heat from the stove is lovely. Why is it different to the heat from an electric heater? Why do I love staring into the flames, and why are these flames alone almost worth my making the trip into the mountains?

Fire has an ancient history. Our forefathers, *Homo erectus*, learned to control fire as early as two million years ago. Remains of a fire dating back 500,000 years have been found in China. And fire was more important back then. Important for keeping wild animals away, important for staying warm, important for cooking, drying clothes, being able to see. Important for good stories, good conversations. Fire remains popular, with almost all new houses having at least one fireplace. We don't have one in our flat in Oslo, so the stove here is one of the reasons I love coming. I find the flames comforting.

I also find the knowledge that I could go back home tomorrow comforting. I could. No one is forcing me to stay here. I try to think about uplifting things, like how nature has more natural light to offer than just daylight. Milky seas, for example. This luminous blue phenomenon can only be seen during the night when the sea is in motion and small species of plankton release the light they have absorbed during the day. There are also bioluminescent beetles – and lightning from clear or pitch-black skies. Not to mention bioluminescent fungi, of which several different species have been discovered. Then there are the northern lights and the moon and all the stars. I know they're there even though it's overcast right now. Even deep down at the bottom of the sea, in the depths of the Mariana Trench, almost 11,000 metres beneath the surface of the ocean, where you would expect it to be dark, it's not. There are creatures there that emit light, plants and jellyfish and other creatures that glow in the dark. That's a comforting thought, right?

I've locked the door. I'm still sitting on the sofa, wrapped in the woollen blanket, crocheting small granny squares in red and yellow and orange and brown that will eventually be sewn together to make a big blanket, thinking and thinking and thinking. Sometimes it's too much, too muddled, with too many thoughts colliding. Big thoughts and questions about the universe and its darkness and the fear, and whether there's any point to it all, collide – bang – with trivial thoughts and questions about luminescent plankton and fireplaces. Maybe I should paint the walls a lighter colour.

Ugh, all this thinking! What a curse. Our intelligent brains are perhaps the main reason why we are well on our way to destroying nature, the basis of our own existence. Paradoxically, we now need to use those same brains to find the solutions necessary to save the world. Climate pessimism won't help, at any rate.

Time to break out my special trick for emergency situations. This trick is very different to and somewhat less sophisticated than hours of meditation. But the aim is the same: to switch off and quell uncontrolled thought chaos, thought storms that tear and ravage; thought artillery that bombards you with unsolved problems, logistics, memories, sorrow, joy, endlessly repeating itself – and never giving you peace.

Meditation exercises are linked to both physical and mental relaxation. And the benefits of clearing your mind are legion:

peace, better concentration, greater insight and a better understanding of the world and of yourself.

My trick for getting to sleep isn't as sophisticated. My trick is three words: 'let it go'. Yep, that's it. Let it go. When I know I need to go to sleep, no matter where I am or who I'm with, every time a new thought or twenty threatens to enter my head, that's what I think. Let it go. It's night-time, you can't do anything now, not until tomorrow, you know that, Sigri.

And then I go to sleep. There on the sofa, wrapped in the woollen blanket, fully dressed. Unbelievable.

The link between night and darkness

The Norwegian Meteorological Institute defines night as the period between midnight and 06:00, and I think that's sensible. Other explanations are just confusing. I find definitions stating that night is the time when an area of the Earth is turned away from the sun, making it dark, misleading. This suggests, for example, that Svalbard doesn't have nights from the beginning of April until the end of August. Or doesn't have days from November until February. This suggests that the North Pole and the South Pole only have one night and one day a year.

But it's hard to deny that night and darkness are linked. They just are. And I sleep. In the very deepest phase, early in

26

the night, when it's almost impossible to remember any of your dreams.

Night

It's this time of the day
when the heavens have gone to hell

and the entire rotary mechanism creaks
walls and ceilings
groan and screech

it's no dream
each of these hours
is deeper than the darkness

and I don't count for anything

Sonja Nyegaard

I wake up in the middle of the night. Undress, brush my teeth, crawl into bed. Try to go back to sleep.

Sleep like hell

When I had my first child, I did postnatal exercises in an attempt to train up my muscles, including my pelvic floor. What I remember best is the instructor saying: 'If you ever have to choose between sleeping or exercising, sleep!' She laughed as she said it, and we chuckled as well.

I'll never forget five particular words from a book we new mums and dads read about the postnatal period and how everything was suddenly so different and overwhelming. A couple in the most intense period of their child's infancy are lying in bed chatting, presumably late at night, and they know they should be sleeping instead, so their conversation ends with these words that I still repeat to those who need them as often as I can: 'Sleep now, sleep like hell'.

Because our relationship with sleep changes fundamentally once we've had kids. Now it's as if I can never get enough of it, even though they're growing and growing and very rarely wake me up at night any more.

Sleep is free – medicine without side effects. We spend over a third of our lives asleep. We're designed to have enough energy for approximately one day before our bodies need to rest. Some people refer to wakefulness as an overload of the brain that can be corrected by sleep. Normally, adults need around seven hours of sleep a night. Children and I need more. Definitely more.

When we sleep, we don't need food; we conserve energy, our body temperature falls by between 1 and 1.5 degrees, our pulse slows and our heart rate decreases slightly. This gives our bodies the peace that they need to do other things, including repairing tissue and other damaged parts, flushing and rebuilding brain cells, storing memories, forgetting things that don't matter, getting rid of waste and conditioning blood vessels so that they don't harden. Sleep also regulates our appetite and boosts the conversion of sugar and fat in our bodies, and is crucial for coping with the day ahead, with work, school – with life itself.

Because there is a strong link between lack of sleep, stress and immune defence.

Inability to sleep used to be considered a symptom of another underlying problem. Researchers now agree that if you are unable to sleep, this in itself can make you ill. If we don't get enough sleep, we become more susceptible to conditions such as Type 2 diabetes, and sometimes we gain weight.

For example, night shifts, which often lead to less sleep and a disrupted circadian rhythm – a natural, internal process that regulates the sleep-wake cycle and repeats roughly every 24 hours – have been linked to stroke, heart attack and some forms of cancer.

29

We also remember less, find it more difficult to concentrate and are less able to tackle complicated tasks if we do not get enough sleep. And it has an effect on our mood.

After only six days of four hours of sleep a night, research subjects had a completely different composition of hormones, with profiles comparable to those of very elderly people – and people with depression.

Lord help me. That's just how it is. If you can't sleep, you're likely to experience a multitude of problems, both physical and mental.

A report from 2009 states that 30 per cent of us sometimes have trouble sleeping, while 10 per cent always do – and this figure seems to be increasing. Four years later, studies were conducted demonstrating that young people aged between sixteen and nineteen spend much longer getting to sleep than before, and that they generally sleep two hours less than they themselves think they need – just over six hours a night on weekdays. Doctors are also prescribing more and more medication for those who are unable to sleep. Norwegian researchers believe that trouble sleeping is now so widespread it constitutes a public health issue. Others refer to it as a global epidemic. In Australia, the number of people reporting trouble sleeping has increased to between 35 and 45 per cent of the population, and a study shows that this costs Australian society almost 45 billion Australian dollars – approximately 25 billion pounds sterling – a year.

So what is the reason for this? Why can't we sleep? Of course, sleeplessness has many different causes – but might it also have something to do with all this artificial light?

I do my best to fall asleep. My mobile flashes and lights up. I should really switch it off. I close my eyes.

The long, deep winter sleep

When I was pregnant for the second time, it was autumn, and I was so nauseous I just wanted to hibernate. Like a pregnant polar bear, who sleeps away the darkness of winter and only re-emerges once the cubs are born and the light has returned.

Over 90 per cent of all animals in Norway – so almost all of them – sleep through the winter. This applies to everything that is unable to fly south to where it is sunny and warm, or to manage in some other way. Animals hibernate because it's cold and dark, because there is limited access to food and water, and quite simply to avoid all the stress that winter entails for small or vulnerable creatures. And they do it by reducing their energy consumption.

The transition between deep sleep and hibernation is gradual.

The deeper the hibernation, the lower the energy consumption and body temperature – and the slower the pulse. True hibernators can lower their body temperature to 2 degrees and slow their pulse to two beats a minute and their metabolism to a minimum. Hibernation can last for up to seven months.

This means it's important for them to find a nice, cosy place to sleep. The common brimstone butterfly, for example, can find a home in small holes and cracked tree trunks. It is one of few species of butterfly that is fully developed in the autumn and overwinters as a fully fledged individual.

The viper hunkers down with its fellows, preferably under tree roots or between rocks on a mountain slope. Together they manage to stay warm. But if the weather suddenly warms up, for example in January, the vipers may slither out, and then, if it suddenly gets cold again, they don't stand a chance. They can't tolerate more than half an hour of frost before it's game over.

Bats hang upside down in old shelters or caves. They hang there and hibernate all winter, their body temperature dropping down towards freezing but staying high enough that they don't freeze solid in deepest winter.

Female bears need a good den to ensure a deep sleep, whereas males need only lie close to a pine trunk with adequate foliage to provide protection. Conversely, their cousin in the north, the polar bear, is a predator with access to food in the winter, which means they don't need to hibernate. Male polar bears roam around for the duration of the polar night. The female polar bear, on the other hand, digs a snow hole and hibernates when darkness descends in the north. She stays there until the transition between February and March, when the light returns. When she finally emerges, it is with one or two cubs in tow which she has breastfed and looked after for the duration of the long Arctic winter. Polar bear cubs only weigh about half a kilo when they are born and are completely naked – with no fur at all. Their mother serves as a mattress and duvet for them for months.

I have discussed hibernators with zoologist Petter Bøckman. And I was compelled to ask:

'What about humans? Wouldn't it be good for us to hibernate as well?'

'We're subtropical, diurnal animals with regular access to food, so we only need to sleep at night, during which time our body temperature drops a little as well. The dark tricks us into believing we need more sleep in the winter, but we don't really,' he says.

I think about how many common brimstones will be waking up this spring. Humans have wiped out many larger species of animal through the ages, and now we're affecting the Earth more than ever before, we're in the process of putting an end to smaller species as well.

Let it go, I think to myself, *insects too*. But my trick for getting to sleep doesn't always work. I have a quick look at my phone. I've figured out how to put it in night mode, which means the screen emits a softer, yellower light. It's supposed to help make sure the light doesn't leave you wide awake. But it's still best to switch it off, even I know that. I pull myself together and do just that. Then I need to pee.

Christiane

Christiane and the trappers more or less hibernate in Gråhuken. During the darkest period, after Christmas, in early January. When everything around them is unpleasant and dead, and their cabin is enveloped in silence and darkness.

'It occurs to me that the long night is only just beginning, and it is as if all my courage might desert me. Maybe the sun will not return at all. Maybe all the world is dark.' She writes that the days pass uneventfully, without any real work to be done and without liberating glimpses of reality. She writes that they lie there at night, not tired but not completely awake either, just surrounded by the eternal darkness and deep silence. And in this physical state of hibernation, their minds start to wander.

Early in the morning she hears the coffee grinder. The sound starts to pull her out of her torpor, but she is not sure whether this is a blessing or a curse. Either way, slowly she comes to and realises that a new day has begun.

DAY 2

Tuesday

DAY 2

Tuesday

It's dark when I wake up on Tuesday and I realise I must have dropped off in the end. I feel like I've been asleep for a long time. I don't know what time it is. Oddly, the morning darkness is kinder than the evening darkness. I don't know why; perhaps because I'm awake and intending to get up and go out. I'm not tired, not scared. I decide to stay here for one more day. At least. I decide my fear has taken up more than enough space up here and I need to try and pull myself together. There are still some embers in the stove, so it's easy to build back up.

Winter Morning

When I woke up this morning there was ice on
    the windows,
but I basked in the glow of a lovely dream.
And the stove pushed warmth out into the room
from a log it had been savouring all night long.

Olav H. Hauge,
translated by Siân Mackie

Now I'm ready for whatever might happen. Almost no matter what. It's strange how we go from one extreme to the other. The heat from the stove is warming the room. I eat crispbread with cod roe for breakfast. Make coffee. Look out at the black and white landscape. There's not much obstructing the view here, so this is what I see from the window: a frozen lake, rocks, snow, Hardanger Glacier and grey sky with clouds rolling east, not too fast, not too slow, at a pace that is just right. There are other small cabins close to this one, dotted around the landscape. No one has been allowed to build here since the 1970s, and there are strict rules on what can be built, how big it can be and building methods, which is good. That's why there aren't any water mains or big luxury cabins here. And on a weekday like today, and during off-season, there aren't any people here either. Not a ski track in sight. Overcast, mild breeze, a few degrees below zero. I finish eating, put on my ski boots, ski trousers with braces, jacket, hat, snood, gloves. Go outside to greet the day with my new-found courage.

Christiane

When Christiane was travelling north by boat, a man gave her his best piece of advice for spending the winter in Svalbard: 'Go for a walk every day, even when it's dark all the time and when there are storms. It's as important as eating and drinking. Keep your spirits up. Never doubt, by which I mean don't be disheartened! Then you'll be fine, just fine.' And Christiane Ritter follows his advice. She walks every day, bent almost double by the end and when the weather is poor. She often walks alone, preferring to head south, inland along the fjord. Because that was where she last saw the sun, and that is where it will reappear in four months.

We need daylight

Exercise is ancient medicine. The government recommends a brisk, thirty-minute walk two to three times a week. And what's interesting is that research shows exercise is particularly beneficial if you go from doing nothing at all to doing just a little. I'll try to sum this up in a few short sentences, since it's all fairly obvious and becoming increasingly clear from research as well: when we exercise, we are happier, healthier, remember more, sleep better, learn more effectively, digest things better and fall ill less often. Some people say they have their best ideas while walking. Others say it lifts the veil over their eyes. There are people who walk their way out of depression, out of their own darkness. I often walk myself out of bad moods. The world and everyday life make more sense after a walk, and sometimes I just need to move.

It's also a way of exposing yourself to daylight.

Light and dark are essential for our circadian rhythm, and this has been the case since the dawn of time – since the Earth started orbiting the sun and day and night came to be. All living organisms have adapted to the way the light changes throughout the day and across the seasons. Our circadian rhythm means we need both day and night, light and dark, activity and rest. And since we're subtropical, diurnal – that is to say, non-nocturnal – animals, we're not designed for summers with no dark, and definitely not for the Nordic winter. We need darkness during the summer, and we need daylight during the winter. The sun, with its heat and energy, is the foundation of all life on Earth. It is five billion years old, and we're lucky, because it still has enough fuel for about as many billion years more.

Daylight is defined as direct sunlight, diffuse sky radiation and light reflected by the Earth and terrestrial objects. When the light reaches our retina, photosensitive nerve cells are activated that send a signal to the brain, triggering the production of stimulants such as the hormone cortisol.

Daylight is also an important source of vitamin D. This means that getting the right amount of light is important. Too little light can lead to mood swings, depression, lack of energy, trouble sleeping and poor impulse control.

Researchers say that it is good to have a kitchen window that faces east so that you are guaranteed a dose of daylight with your breakfast. You can also buy blinds that are designed to let light through to you and your bed so that you can wake up to the morning sun and birdsong. And there are daylight lamps you can set up on your desk when it's always dark.

Because despite our light summers, studies show that there is a lot less direct sunlight here in Scandinavia than at other latitudes. This is because of the cloud cover, which means that we rarely have clear skies, and the fact that the sun hangs low in the sky – only between 0 and 10 degrees above the horizon – for 35 per cent of the year.

This suggests direct sunlight is hard to come by for more than a third of the year. And if you live in the shadow of a hill or in a town with many buildings, you might not get any direct sunlight when the sun is low in the sky. For the sake of comparison, the sun is only that low in Madrid for 10 per cent of the year.

We also build towns differently now. In days gone by, it was important for daylight to get in because there wasn't any electricity, and when electricity was finally harnessed, it was expensive and not widely available.

But daylight and sun are like a lot of other things: you need some, but too much isn't good. Too much might result in sunburn, skin cancer, snow blindness, water blindness – and madness.

The big white light

There are stories about people who went mad in Svalbard, but it wasn't during the polar night that they snapped – it was when the light returned in the spring. During the summer. The midnight sun hangs in the sky twenty-four hours a day as soon as 19 April in Longyearbyen. At first it's nice, when it looks like it's bobbing on the surface of the sea, painting the clouds and sky pink and purple, but as summer draws in, it rises higher and higher into the sky, becoming a white orb that just keeps circling and circling, draining the life and colour from everything.

One of the first things we learned up there was to smear washing-up liquid on the bedroom windows and put up aluminium foil so that less of the relentless summer light could get in. So that we could sleep.

I've heard stories from Northern Norway as well, about how during the war most Germans were sent home when the light returned, in the spring, in the summer. In the time of the big white light.

In such long summer light or winter darkness, our rhythm can be disturbed. Seasonal affective disorder was a psychological diagnosis for a long time. New research shows it's a bit more complicated, with each person's 'light history' being important. But the basic premise still applies: people need both light and darkness to function – and preferably in the right doses. So what are the right doses, and what effect does artificial light have on our rhythm?

Christiane

Christiane carries their laundry to the stream to rinse it out. She has skis on her feet, a stick in one hand and the tub in the other. She moves slowly into the autumn, into the dark. 'The deep silence is like a heavy blanket over nature, and the snow on the ground dampens every sound. [...] The world has fallen into deep dusk from which it can no longer rise.'

43

Unsafe ice and a sad home-alone party

I put on my skis. Glide down towards the lake covered by snow and ice. All the streams have frozen over for the winter. Ordinarily we cut a hole in the ice to collect water, but it's still early in the season, not even Christmas yet, and I'm not sure whether the ice is safe. I give it a thump with one of my ski poles, but I don't dare walk on it.

Ice on lakes is unpredictable, and there is a lot to remember when assessing how safe it is. Be wary of ice where rivers begin and end; be wary of fresh snow on the ice; be wary along shorelines and by wharves and in narrow straits; be wary around islands, headlands and where plants and trees are growing through the ice; be wary of big rocks.

There's also a lot to remember when walking on the ice. Any give, creaking, cracks and surface water can be signs of unsafe ice. As can milky-white ice and darker sections of ice.

One December a few years ago, a friend and I were walking across the lake Finsevatnet. We were going to the railway station and following ski tracks that someone else had made. We were talking. But then, mid-sentence, amid flurries of snowflakes and laughter, in the middle of the day, in the middle of the lake, half-way between the cabin and the station, in the wind at -4 degrees, one of my skis suddenly sank. I barely had time to process this before my other ski was underwater as well. I couldn't feel anything beneath my feet, so I grabbed for the edge of the ice and started treading water with my skis.

I managed to keep my head. I've read and written about falling through the ice before, so I know the theory. I know I only have a few minutes before my body starts going numb. I know I mustn't panic.

The body's alarm system is activated when you are truly afraid. Ready to fight or run. This gave me the strength to hold on and think clearly.

My friend lay down and reached out to me with her ski pole. The edge of the ice was surprisingly sturdy and I managed to climb out with my skis on. I was wet from my toes to my throat.

We ran just under a kilometre back to the cabin. To dry off and talk about it.

I read a lot and spoke to a lot of people after that. My theory now is that there wasn't any ice under the fresh snow at all. Perhaps because there was a big rock there and the wind direction meant no ice had formed. Or perhaps watercourse regulation meant the water level had dropped. How can you prepare yourself for a shock like falling through the ice?

According to experts, you can't. Nevertheless, it helps to jump into ice-cold water under controlled conditions, because this helps make certain actions automatic so that hopefully your body will remember them when they're needed in serious situations. It helps to know that everything will probably be okay. And that if you are completely submerged beneath the ice and cannot find the hole again, it will still be light enough for you to see. The ice is light, so you need to look for and swim towards the darkest point. The darkest point might be your salvation.

And this is so important: do not romanticise nature. Don't attribute so much good to it that you forget to be prepared, forget the weather report and common sense and good advice and to carry what you need in your bag, and most important of all: know your limits.

Because no matter how good nature makes us feel, no matter how much we try to lose ourselves in and harness and conquer and become one with mountain and fjord and plateau and forest and sea, it's still unbridled nature. It doesn't care whether you're kind or cruel, beautiful or ugly, clever or stupid, thin or fat. Nature doesn't judge you, assess you, like people and society do. It doesn't give you likes or loves or wows. And there is something really wonderful and liberating about that, about not being seen. But nature's indifference to us doesn't mean that those who are not well enough prepared avoid punishment.

There is a picture of my mother and me in the cabin visitors' book in Finse. I must have been five or six years old. Above the picture it says: 'The home-alone party that ended in tears'. My mother used to tell me that story all the time, and now she tells it to my children. The story of when I wanted to stay home alone while my parents and my little brother went to the railway station. The weather was nice and there were bananas I could eat if I got hungry. And water I could drink if I got thirsty.

I was happy and looked forward to being alone. I remember thinking that if all went well I'd soon be able to leave home – or at least I could if I wanted to. I had a similar notion when I learned to slice bread. Now I'm all grown up. Now I can look after myself without Mum and Dad's help. No problem. Life's a party.

But something made me change my mind. My mum says I was scared I'd starve, scared they would never come back, scared of all sorts of things and of dying there alone. So I got dressed, shoes on the wrong feet and my hat on askew, and then I set out, crying and alone, in the direction of the station. There was snow on the ground, but I can't remember whether I was wearing skis. I'd have to ask my mum.

The need of the pack animal to be alone

And here I am again, all alone. I'm better prepared this time, and I know it's something I have to do. I've become more sensitive

47

to crowds and noise and different atmospheres over the years. I need quiet.

Some people say that venturing out into and turning to nature is a means of withdrawing from what is important. I think seeking out nature and paying it heed is actually the opposite – it's like coming home or going back to basics. To what we're all an important part of, to what we really need to be talking about now, if we and the Earth are to stand a chance.

As I have often heard legendary outdoorsman Nils Faarlund say: 'It's too late to be pessimistic.'

In any case, I need to get away from all the noise and spend some time alone. I need air and space, and to make sense of the dark.

But humans are pack animals, so I need people as well. There's something paradoxical about how we need to be alone as much as we need others. We might carry them with us in our thoughts and memories, no matter what happens. And nowadays, when true wilderness is almost a thing of the past and technology allows messages and snaps and updates to trickle and pour in, and satellite phones work wherever we are – are we *ever* alone?

Well, this works for me. I'm physically alone, I'm warm and full, and it's still light outside. And the internet coverage here is abysmal, so I'm unlikely to be bothered.

I return from my short afternoon walk without water, because of the whole unsafe ice thing. I fill buckets with snow from a drift outside to melt in the big pot inside. I haven't seen any people today either. I've read a little, heated up some fishcakes and vegetables for lunch, tidied some shelves and played records on the old record player, but I haven't done half of what I'd intended to.

It feels like the second day is drawing to a close here in the mountains. Much too quickly. Because it's already getting dark. I sit in the same place as yesterday. On the sofa, with the blanket. Fire up the stove, crochet a yellow and red granny square and let it come.

It's still bluish-grey outside. I go out to pee and see that one of the neighbouring cabins has an outside light on even though they're not here. It's kind of reassuring, but it's terrible too. Irritating. And there's no law against it – not yet.

Wondering whether I'll get scared is making me feel anxious. I consider switching on a light in the cabin, but decide to wait.

Artificial light

Humans started by lighting fires and torches. Then, ten thousand years ago, they started burning oil in containers. Animal fat, plant oil and petroleum were used as fuel over the years. Oil lamps were the main source of artificial light until science really figured out electricity. Gas was used for a while before lamps were finally lit using electric energy. The first electric lights, carbon arc lamps, emerged in around 1850, providing a bright light that was sometimes used for outside lighting. Then came the carbon filament lamp, which was better suited to general use.

Then renowned American inventor Thomas Alva Edison invented the incandescent lamp, which had a long service life, and also developed ways of supplying the public with electricity.

Skien was the first city in Norway to make electric light available to the public, in 1885. Hammerfest was the first town in the world to have artificial street lights following a fire in 1889. Valen Hospital in Sunnhordland was the first hospital in the Nordic region to be supplied with electric power, in 1910. The Royal Palace and a church in Oslo were the only public buildings to have electric power before this.

But it was only after 1950 that most Norwegian homes had electric lights. This was a game changer in a country with such dark winters. Because that's been our biggest problem as long as I can remember: too little light in the winter.

When the incandescent lamp was introduced, our sleep was reduced by an average of one and a half hours. The EU banned these lamps in 2012, and since LED bulbs are much more energy-efficient, there are lights on everywhere now, twenty-four hours a day, all year round. Outside and inside. All the same, more electricity was used in Norway in 2017 than ever before. And sleep disorders are on the rise.

Light pollution and night sky laws

When I lived in Longyearbyen, I could go hiking in the mountains nearby at any hour during the polar night without a headlamp because of how brightly lit the town was with all its street lights. The tower block where we live in the city is never completely dark either, no matter the season. In the evenings, my kids disappear out on to the balcony as soon as I tear them away from their screens. They like to sleep out there. And even though it's not completely dark, even though we can't see the Milky Way, we can still see some stars. We can see the Big Dipper above the building next door at bedtime, and my eldest has named a star after himself. And every morning they sit there, ruddy-cheeked, with bowls of muesli, after sleeping through city noise and dogs barking and parties in the building next door. But the amount of light in the local area has increased in the last year. The balcony is no longer safe from bright outdoor lights. The stars are becoming harder to see, and the more I learn about this, the more uneasy I feel as a mother.

There are few places left in the world that are not polluted by artificial light. Pictures taken by NASA show that light pollution has increased dramatically in the last twenty years. Light pollution is defined as *excessive and inappropriate artificial light*, and researchers are now discovering more and more areas where this light is causing harm.

Almost all types of pollution are regulated in Norway: air and noise, and what can be discharged into sea, fresh water and earth. According to section 6(3) of the Norwegian Pollution Control Act, light is only to be considered pollution 'to the extent determined by the pollution control authority'. And according to Norwegian lawyer Erling Fjeldaas, no measures have been taken to counteract light pollution since the act entered into force in 1981. He is incensed that everyone is free to create as much artificial light pollution as they like, with few exceptions. In his prizewinning master's thesis, he discusses Norwegian legislation in this area, finding both frighteningly few regulations and frighteningly few examples of complaints about excessive artificial light being taken seriously. For example, in the Norwegian Planning and Building Act and in civil engineering regulations there are no application requirements concerning light specifically. Many municipalities therefore misinterpret this as meaning people do not need permission to erect lamp posts.

When three huge floodlights were erected to illuminate a mountainside in Rjukan, a neighbour complained about the indirect light encroaching on her property. She described the case as 'emotional abuse on the part of the business, which failed to involve people in a project that would have such a significant effect on their lives and mental health'. The county governor in Telemark ruled that permission was not required to erect the floodlights. Fjeldaas found paragraphs in both the Constitution and the Norwegian Public Health Act that can be used to protect people from light trespass. Among other things, section 14(1) of the Norwegian Public Health Act states: 'The municipality may order that aspects of a property or activities in the municipality be rectified if the situation has a direct or indirect negative impact on health […]'.

In Arendal, there were complaints about a huge screen displaying adverts and information about the city. The light from the screen was reflected by the sea, and the city's neighbours on the other side of the fjord found the light unpleasant, claiming it made it difficult for them to sleep. The Public Health Act could also have been cited here, but the complainants did not win their case in this instance either.

Doctors across the country are hearing more and more complaints about the use of bright and unpleasant light at night. Many people are told they should just close their curtains and then it will be dark. But the authorities do have the power to make a difference. In a rare decision in 2009, Ålesund Municipality forbade SK Herd, a sports club, from using outdoor lighting after nine o'clock in the evening, and they also stipulated rules on how bright the light could be.

Other countries have proven more concerned about preserving the night sky than Norway. An organisation called the Dark Sky Association is fighting for this, and eighteen American states have adopted laws against light pollution. In New Mexico, for example, all bulbs brighter than 150 watts must be shielded, and if they are not, they must be switched off from eleven o'clock at night until sunrise. Some states have done so much to preserve the night sky that tourists and stargazers are now flocking there to experience the darkness. The organisation is also working on preserving the darkness in parks and other landscapes. They have certified thirty-five places around the world so far, and in the autumn of 2018 a large national park in France, Cévennes National Park, was made an International Dark Sky Reserve, thereby becoming the biggest park in Europe to have achieved this status.

Germany has also started discussing this, and extensive dimming of outdoor lighting in public spaces has been introduced in some towns. On the Spanish island of La Palma, there is a law they refer to as the 'Sky Law', which regulates the light. This was introduced because there is an important astronomical observatory – where work does not really start until after dark – high up on a mountain on the island for which natural darkness is a necessity. Other observatories around the world have been rendered useless simply because they have not managed to shut out the steadily increasing light pollution. The sky shines yellowish-brown at night and reflects all artificial light sources. But in La Palma, those who break the Sky Law face large fines. Among other things, the brightness of all street lights is reduced by 50 per cent at midnight, making the light softer and more orange. And all the lights point down at the ground.

The Dark Sky Association has specific advice on how to speak to neighbours and public bodies about having unpleasant light dimmed. They talk about a global movement for the starry sky. Being able to experience true night, a starry sky in all its glory, is a human right. It's a lovely thought.

Erling Fjeldaas is fighting to bring such legislation to Norway as well. He has specific proposals for amendments to laws, and wants the lighting used by sports centres, hothouses, aquaculture facilities and roads to be regulated and outdoor lighting requirements to be stipulated in civil engineering regulations. 'The rules should concern the angle of the light, the brightness of the light and when the light is switched on [...] Unfortunately, our view of the sky has not yet been discussed in the Norwegian Parliament. The parties ought to have opinions on this,' he writes.

We need natural darkness

Another Norwegian, the journalist Erlend Christian Lysvåg, is worried about what we miss out on in an excessively lit world: '[...] artificial light makes night, darkness and all the innumerable nuances of nature's own light inaccessible to us. We don't see stars, don't see the animals, the shadows, the distinctive details that emerge from the darkness. We have effectively stunted our sensory perception and would no longer cope if the power suddenly cut out for good. We are unable to orientate ourselves, unable to navigate – unable to live, really,' he writes.

And the situation is critical. Two thirds of Norwegians now live where they are unable to see the Milky Way. New studies show that 60 per cent of Europeans and 80 per cent of North Americans cannot see it either.

More and more tourists are coming to Norway to experience the polar night, northern lights and starry sky – and the silence. We Norwegians brag about our untainted nature and lovely mountains and fjords, but even so, a greyish-yellow veil has been drawn over large parts of our country and some of the best we have to offer.

Municipal autonomy in Norway means that the municipalities do not need to wait for the state to take action and can step in themselves. This means it is possible to regulate all light, to consider what needs light and when – and what type of light is used. There might well be places hoping to become Norway's first Starry Sky Preserve or Dark Sky Community. Places where, in the event of a particularly good weather or northern lights report during the winter, a star alarm could sound and all unnecessary light could be switched off for a while to allow everyone to look up and out into the universe itself.

Such a thing would be beautiful and important, saving more than just energy and money. Natural darkness is about so much more than experiencing nature. Researchers are finding more and more evidence to suggest that too much artificial light can have a detrimental effect on our bodies, rhythms and mood. And we're not the only ones who are affected. It has an impact on other animals and the ecosystem, too – on nature itself.

We need natural darkness.

Christiane

Total darkness descends on Gråhuken. Christiane writes that the darkness has now confined them to the cabin. All three of them take turns doing the housework, otherwise keeping busy with various things. Hermann writes and reads, she repairs clothes, and Karl 'always has something that needs building, soldering or putting together'. They play solitaire and tell stories, all while the world outside is consumed by night. They do not dare venture far from the cabin in such deep darkness.

'The storms, which sometimes last for days, are really all that is left of reality, and at night, when it is quiet in the cabin, they are what command our consciousness.'

I fear the Wanderer

If you were to ask me what I'm afraid of up here in the mountains, I'd probably tell you it's what I can't see but might be there anyway. I'm scared someone will come up to the window, scare me, break down the door, attack me. Scared of vagrants with dirty beards and no fixed abode who don't like people and break into the cabins they come across, who suddenly appear from who knows fucking where with torches and axes. After all, the world isn't always a nice place, and these things do happen. There are women from other countries, war-ridden countries, who have had bad experiences of being removed from civilisation, because out in the countryside they were easy targets. Our interest in outdoor pursuits is probably incomprehensible to them, and understandably so.

Something terrible happens every day, every second, even in Norway, kidnapping and murder and assault and disappearances and, well, I suppose animals are merciless too, and nature is indifferent, but no one – *no one* – is as disrespectful as so-called human beings.

I was afraid of the Wanderer for years.

He grew up in Bergen. His family loved the great outdoors. He wanted to be a football player. He went to Copenhagen to play, but ended up homeless. He later became part of the drug scene in Bergen, and after that he wandered, and wandered, and wandered.

He roamed the mountains around Voss in the 1980s before heading further east. He broke into over a thousand cabins, and he was convicted of 664 of those break-ins. He would break a window or break down the door. Steal small things like fishing equipment, comic books, soup, sauerkraut, shoes, bags, stoves, maps, books. Food and alcohol. He sometimes defecated on the floor before he went on his way.

He hid and ran from the police, from his past and from furious cabin owners in Hallingdal, Gudbrandsdalen and the areas surrounding Lake Mjøsa. And every time he was caught and locked up, he promised he would stop. He was in prison for years. He later said he didn't really want to keep wandering around, but that it was difficult to stop now he'd started.

'No one has provoked the ire of so many district sheriffs since storehouse thief Gjest Baardsen in the 19th century. Some of the police officers who have searched for him laugh when we call: "Tell him to get in touch if you find him, won't you? I don't know how many man hours we've spent on him. He runs for the hills as soon as the sun comes out in the spring, and then he lets himself be caught when the snow comes. He has animal instincts and knows the terrain like the back of his hand".' This was reported in the newspaper *Aftenposten* in 2005.

The Wanderer waited for night to fall before he started walking. He walked where he couldn't be seen, avoiding paths, roads and bridges where he risked running into other people. He was afraid in the light and safe in the dark. He knew no one would find him in the dark because they would all be asleep. The darkness was his friend.

It sounds like a lonely life to me, but the Wanderer once said in an interview that he liked walking alone. The journalist asked what motivated him. 'Alcohol. Once I've started drinking, it's difficult to stop,' explained Terje Larsen, which was his actual name.

He went on to say he could drink up to three litres of spirits a day. His night vision became poorer when he drank, but he never drank so much that he was unable to walk.

The police said he was harmless, but a lot of people were angry. Cabin owners said that if they caught him they would beat him. Others were more sympathetic. Because there's something quite romantic about simply walking, and when you think about it, the Wanderer was just doing what humans have always done: walking around looking for what he needed to survive and keep going. His instincts and senses were more developed than most. He was very sensitive to sounds, smells, changes. Like an animal.

Sight has gradually become the most important sense for most of us, perhaps even to the extent that it hinders our other senses, our perception. Perhaps the Wanderer stirred something in us that has long lain dormant. How long would you survive out there? Completely alone in nature? Maybe he tapped into something primordial that has been lost to most modern humans.

The Wanderer had no pack. He said as much himself. That he was a lone wolf.

Christiane

Christiane is alone in the cabin in Gråhuken. She spends a lot of time alone when the men are busy working. Back then, fewer than 10 per cent of those who spent the winter trapping in Svalbard were women, and very few of them participated actively in the trapping.

Christiane sits in the cabin and tries to concentrate on her sewing. She sews and repairs things, and she also draws and paints watercolours. She is an artist, after all. But her reasons for keeping herself occupied are not as obvious as one might think. She keeps busy so that she won't have time to think too much, because that would mean dwelling on 'the vast nothingness' outside. And that is not a good idea when she is alone.

'I am wary of the power of thought, which can determine whether a person lives or dies. I sense – indeed, I know for certain – that it was fear of the vast nothingness that caused the deaths of so many people in Spitsbergen in centuries gone by.'

She writes that it was not just scurvy that killed them. They often died even if they had enough food and weapons and animals to hunt. But some of them did not dare venture outside. Fear waited just outside the door, reaching across the desolate landscape like a monster.

'It was the image of total desolation, of this horrific standstill, that had taken root in their minds and sapped their energy, stealing their strength.'

I need comfort

Many of the trappers in Svalbard were there all alone. Some of them admitted that they went there to avoid ending up in a psychiatric hospital. Up and out into the big, white freedom on the plateaus.

But it can all become too much. One trapper used to call the Governor of Svalbard when he'd had enough and ask for someone to come and collect him so that he could get professional help in Tromsø.

The Wanderer, Terje Larsen, wasn't afraid of the dark. Of the vast nothingness. But I'm convinced that he was afraid of something. The more I read about him, the more I want to talk to him.

But towards the end of my work on this book, I discover that he has been found dead. Outside a cabin he had broken into. The people who find him call a doctor, and a helicopter comes, but they can't save him. The Wanderer was sixty years old.

It's completely dark here in the mountains now, and with the darkness comes the fear, even though I know it's irrational. It's still only Tuesday, but I'm ready to go home now. To my kids and my husband and the city. Yes, I'm scared of people, but now I'm scared of other things too, of thinking more and too much, of chasms and fissures opening up, and of black holes in my consciousness pulling me down, sucking me in. Everyone has something that threatens to swallow them, be it divorce, illness, sorrow or some other dark devilry, and oh look, now I'm using those metaphors as well, the ones that paint a picture of the dark as something negative. Now I'm scared my imagination will latch on to all this, all these figments, as Christiane calls them, and compound them.

The last vestiges of daylight are gone. I only arrived yesterday, but I might have to go home tomorrow.

Italian researcher Dr Francesco Benedetti, who studies light therapy, says you're not afraid *of* the dark, but *in* the dark. Just like rats are terrified *in* the light because if they go about their business when they can be seen, they'll be caught and killed.

I need comfort now. More than ever. Is it possible to think of the dark as something kind?

In a Kind Darkness

in a kind darkness
we go in
open our eyes
let a stone
a colour
become something else

Tuesday

in that which is
we disappear

and the colours are purple
in that which is
and disappear
and perhaps the colours are purple

because I know the darkness is kind
and that everything is never the same
is always the same
is you and me
as you go in you go out

and the colours are purple
in that which is
and disappear
and perhaps the colours are purple

because I know the darkness is kind

                                        Jon Fosse

Artists and the darkness

Jon Fosse is Norway's greatest writer. His work has been translated into more than fifty languages, and the only Norwegian dramatist whose work is staged more often than his outside Norway is Henrik Ibsen. I send him an email to ask how he would define the word *darkness*. He won't define it for me, but he tells me that it's one of the most important words in his poetry. He writes about *luminous darkness* and *kind darkness*. He writes:

'It goes without saying that darkness has to do with night, with sleep, and with death, and with not being able to see anything, or being able to see stars, in a certain sense being able to see the universe. You can never see further than in the dark. Without darkness there can be no light.'

Fosse writes that in poetry, physical and metaphorical darkness coincide, and: 'Many of the best poets have been broken by their inner darkness'. I think that's well put. I've brought a couple of his books with me to the mountains, and I read:

> And I stood there
> feeling like I was growing emptier and emptier
> that I was empty
> like the rain and the darkness

66

like the wind and the trees
like the sea out there
Now I was no longer anxious
Now I was a great empty calm
Now I was a darkness
a deep darkness
Now I was nothing
And at the same time I felt that
well, that I shone somehow
Deep inside me
from the empty darkness
it was like the empty darkness was shining
[...]

Jon Fosse,
translated by Siân Mackie

The poet Olav H. Hauge didn't let his inner darkness break him. He is one of our greatest poets – certainly the greatest from the post-war period. He was committed for the first time in 1934, to Neevengården Hospital, an asylum in Bergen, when he was only twenty-six years old, despite noticing symptoms four years earlier. He was later admitted to the asylum at Valen Hospital several times as well. His doctors say he had a nervous disorder. He himself refers to it as 'the sorrowful saga of my youth'.

He was later diagnosed with schizophrenia and depression. These disorders affected him in five-year cycles that aligned with his poetry collections being published.

'Olav H. Hauge became so immersed in his reading and writing that he stopped eating, drinking and sleeping. On several occasions, he suffered a breakdown as he was finishing a book. He burned two of his manuscripts shortly after they were completed,' says Knut Olav Åmås, Hauge's biographer.

I could write pages and pages about popular musicians, authors and artists who have delighted the world and enriched our lives with wonderful and important music, art and literature, but who were mentally vulnerable and ended their lives too soon – often through substance misuse – despite receiving a diagnosis and being treated.

There has been research on this. On how certain mental illnesses such as bipolar disorder, previously referred to as manic depression, are more common among artists and those in creative professions. Writers in particular suffer more mental illness than others, with schizophrenia, depression, anxiety and substance misuse occurring frequently in addition to bipolar disorder. According to the same study, writers are almost 50 per cent more likely to take their own lives than other people.

Darkness as a condition

Professor Asle Hoffart taught me about fear of the dark, but in his world inner darkness is primarily linked to pessimism and diagnoses such as depression.

'Feeling and conditions are abstract. That's why they can only be described using metaphors. Nature provides us with many metaphors, for example light and darkness. People who are depressed aren't always able to conceive of their futures, to look forward to anything – for them, the future is dark,' he says.

Between 6 and 12 per cent of Norwegians have been diagnosed with depression, and between 20 and 30 per cent will experience depression at some point in their lives.

'When depression is persistent and severe, it is considered a mental disorder,' Hoffart says. 'It's more than just feeling sad or down at times, more than just feeling anxious and out of sorts, like everyone experiences at some point in their lives.'

It's all of this, just amplified over a longer period of time. Depression is one of the most common health issues in Norway – and globally. The World Health Organisation has concluded that it is one of the leading causes of suffering and functional impairment in the world. The diagnosis can be triggered by something specific in your life, but can also be inherited. It can cause physical symptoms such as pain and exhaustion. Most people with this diagnosis also have anxiety issues.

Depression is generally treated with counselling or medication – or a combination of the two. Medications may contain serotonin, which is a neurotransmitter. Neurotransmitters are messengers that transmit signals across chemical synapses from one nerve cell to another. Serotonin transmits a lot of signals and therefore contributes to everything from how you feel to how you behave – meaning that you need the right amount of this substance to feel happy and secure. A lack of serotonin will make you feel sad, downcast and depressed, and in the worst-case scenario may lead to panic attacks.

'Unfortunately we still know very little about whether the changes in the brain are the reason for the altered experiences or vice versa – or whether parallel processes are at work,' Hoffart says.

But might all this also have something to do with natural and artificial light and darkness? I've heard something about a hormone, a darkness hormone called melatonin, which supposedly plays a very important role in all this – and which is inextricably linked to serotonin. I've been meaning to find out more about it.

Night in the forest

It's dark here in Finse now. The blue hour begins as early as three or four o'clock in the afternoon, hours before I can really justify going to bed. Hours and hours. So many hours that I might as well put the time to good use and come clean: this isn't the first time I've experimented with my fear of the dark; isn't the first time I've tried to embrace and get acquainted with the darkness at this time of year, when it's dark fifteen hours a day.

I wanted to try sleeping alone in the forest one night. I had just moved down from Svalbard to Oslo, a city where mountains are in short supply but there are a lot of trees in a large forest on the city limits. A lot of spruce, a lot of pine. Mostly pine, come to think of it. I like pine best, though, and I wanted to acquaint myself with a big, dense forest typical of those in Eastern Norway, so this seemed like the way to go about it. I asked a friend for advice:

'Think of the darkness as a protector,' he said. 'And besides, what are the chances of someone stumbling over you in the middle of the night?'

One of my friends' teachers once said something similar: 'The darkness isn't your enemy. It's a friend you can hide yourself in.'

I have another friend who has lived alone in the forest for a long time. When he's sitting in his cabin and it gets dark outside and he feels scared, he tells himself, over and over again:

'I'm the scary one. I'm the scary one. Anyone out here will be more afraid of me than I am of them.'

I try to think along the same lines. I tried to think it back then, in the forest, and I try to think it now, in the evening of my second day in the mountains. I'm the scary one, and if anyone comes here now, it'll probably just be because they need shelter or help.

Unless it's the Wanderer. Lurching out of the darkness. What if death isn't enough to stop him walking?

I found a nice spot in the forest and lit a small fire. I had forgone a tent, instead just draping a waterproof poncho over my sleeping bag so that I could look around if I heard anything and thought someone might be coming.

Even then I wasn't scared of wolves or bears or ants in my sleeping bag. I was scared of psychiatric patients on the run, of the Wanderer, of men with shotguns, of characters from horror movies that I never dare watch but who I know often keep to the shadows in the wilderness. I was scared of kids who had been left in the forest to die hundreds of years ago – and who were yet to have their revenge.

I was afraid of people.

*

So I woke up and fell asleep and woke up and fell asleep. I tended the fire so that it wouldn't go out. After a while I didn't know what was a dream and what was reality. A dark shadow fell over me as someone gripped the end of my sleeping bag, trying to drag me away. I jerked awake, reaching for the rifle I always had with me in Svalbard, but which of course I didn't have with me then. There was no one there, and there was no one coming either. I exhaled, trying to calm myself down, trying to get back to sleep. Somehow I managed and took flight.

I have a recurring dream that comes to me night after night: a dream that I can fly. I like flying and I can fly for miles, over mountains, through clouds, to visit friends and family. But sometimes I can't take off, or I can't get high enough. Sometimes, in those dreams, someone is chasing me, trying to catch me. Shadowy figures.

Nightmare: the demon on your chest

The word *nightmare* is derived from *night* + Old English *mære*, or mare. A mare is a terrible, womanlike creature from folklore, a demon that sits on the chests of those who are sleeping and rides them like a horse. And whenever it does this, bad dreams soon follow. The word has the same origin in several languages:

in Norwegian it is *mareritt*, in Swedish *mardröm*, in Icelandic *martröd* and in German *Nachtmahr*.

Dreams are experiences we have when we are asleep, a series of images, thoughts, sounds and sensations that occur in our minds. In our dreams, the line between fantasy and reality becomes blurred. Researchers are yet to say for certain what the function of dreams is, but they have discovered that they originate from a particular area deep inside the back of the brain. This area is also important for processing emotions and visual memory.

Our dreams are at their most vivid during REM sleep. Luckily, during this stage of sleep our muscles are paralysed by a hormone that prevents them from reacting to bad dreams. This hormone has no effect during other stages of sleep, so this is when it becomes possible to sleepwalk and be woken up by your own screams and movements.

Psychologists split our nightmares into several groups. The least dangerous are anxiety dreams, which often occur during REM sleep. These are an unpleasant but somewhat common type of dream about something that doesn't necessarily make sense. As many as 70 per cent of us regularly have bad dreams. Then there are nightmares, which are extremely abstract, grip us more fiercely and cause more pain. A nightmare is often a dream that won't quit, that keeps coming back night after night.

It might be so unpleasant that you feel anxious or scared even after you have woken up.

Then there is night terror, which is a sleep disorder. Those who experience night terror might find that they wake up screaming and moaning in the middle of a severe anxiety attack. It affects 15 per cent of children, starting from the age of two or three. Sufferers often don't wake up completely. Instead, they settle down again and don't remember anything about it when they wake up.

So why do we have nightmares? Researchers aren't entirely sure. There are several theories. One is purely physical, positing that some people's brains have trouble switching from one stage of sleep to another. Another theory is that traumatic events in a person's life can create painful memories that disturb your sleep.

Christiane

In the middle of winter, Christiane sometimes sees a hunched, shadowy figure approaching from the coast: 'Soundlessly it approaches from the troubled waters of the bay down from the cabin, and time and time again I try to free myself from these figments of my imagination.'

Another time, when the other trapper, Karl, has been out hunting on his own in Svendsen Bay, she asks him how it went.

He tells her that no one spends the night there because it is haunted, and then they both laugh.

They know that there is no such thing as ghosts, but they also know that what does not exist can become real in a mind tormented by loneliness and darkness.

Chilling Christmas

When our vision is compromised, our imaginations run wild and we become more aware of things that cannot be seen directly, merely sensed. We celebrate Christmas at the darkest time of year, and it gets darker and darker the further back you go, to a time before electricity, to the good old days. Back then, if you weren't a farmer with significant holdings or some other wealthy sort, you probably didn't have much you could trade for candles and oil lamps. This made Christmas an unnerving time for most people, because the darker and shorter the days became, the more power the otherworldly forces possessed.

Although Norway has celebrated Christmas and light and the birth of Jesus since becoming a Christian country, for a long time the festive season was characterised by dark days, ritual and traditions intended to prevent too much contact with creatures from other worlds, dark forces, ghosts, spirits, the living dead – all such entities that went by various names.

Many of them were associated with the devil and his darkness. All of them were unseen, could do great harm and had a lot of power. It was important to not provoke them. To placate them. To do what they wanted you to do. To not do what they didn't want you to do. They were to be respected.

There were some days and nights during which people had to be particularly careful, days and nights during which all manner of creatures crossed over from the underworld, abandoning their usual posts. Days and nights during which the border between the worlds of men and demons was particularly weak. Such was the case on Lussi Night, Christmas Eve and New Year's Eve – and every Thursday. Thursdays at this time of year were days of rest for the *nisse* – small household sprites from Nordic folklore – which meant it wasn't wise to spin, knit or chop wood.

The night of 13 December was Lussi Night – when Lussi walked the Earth. From the thirteenth century until around 1700, it was widely believed that this was the longest night of the year. This night marked the transition into the polar night, when all the ghosts and trolls and otherworldly creatures were unleashed on the world. But 13 December was also considered the start of the Christmas period, and is still celebrated as the Feast of Saint Lucy, which means this date combines a dark legend with a happy Christian tradition.

Lussi and Lucy

Some people link Lussi in Nordic tradition to Lilith in ancient Jewish tradition. According to this tradition, she was the first woman in the world, created at the same time as the first man, Adam, and long before Eve. She had many children with Adam and is said to have been large and wilful, just like him – preferring to be on top during their sexual encounters. One day, the Lord himself visited the Garden of Eden and wanted to see their children. Lussi heard that He was coming and started washing the children because she didn't want Him to see them while they were dirty. But she didn't have enough time, so she hid them – and refused to present them when the Lord arrived. He didn't like this and banished her and her children from the Garden. They were forced to live underground for eternity, and her children fathered the first demons.

Lussi spent most of her time underground, but around Christmas, when the days were short and the dark forces were at their strongest – that was when she would emerge. And she was invariably furious.

She would ride across the sky on either a broom or a horse. Sometimes she rode alone, sometimes with others. She was as immense as Death and merciless if she found anyone working during the longest night. If you so much as touched a rolling pin, you risked losing a hand. She is even said to have shouted warnings down people's chimneys: 'No brewing, no baking, no unnecessary fire-building'.

Conversely, after the longest night, Lussi liked to make sure that everyone was working hard. After all, there was a lot to be done before Christmas: the beer needed to be brewed, the flatbread made, dust and dirt washed away. During the Christmas period she would separate disobedient children from their parents, and if any adults incurred her wrath, people would be harmed and buildings damaged. However, if she was pleased, she would give the children gifts.

Lussi Night and polar night were dangerous, but it was possible to protect yourself. Tar was used to make sure that woodwork didn't rot, and many people thought it helped protect them from dark forces as well. They would paint tar crosses above their beds and doors, and leave steel scissors and knives on windowsills and by their beds. Sometimes they would even have them *in* their beds. Candles would be lit, and it was just common sense to cut a small cross into anything you baked.

'No cross in the cake and evil spirits partake,' as they used to say.

We now know that 21 December is the longest night, and 13 December is primarily celebrated as the Feast of Saint Lucy in remembrance of the Christian saint. She was killed in around AD 300, a time when Christians were often persecuted for their faith. Lucy means 'as of light', or 'she who shines' – and is good to others.

Sweden started the tradition of the Lucia procession and children carrying candles in 1927. But long before that, centuries before, it was not uncommon for a farmer's eldest daughter to get up early, put on a white dress and walk with a candle through the barn and cowshed and around the entire house. She would stop to sing a magical verse at every corner, the idea being that the light from the candle and her beautiful voice would chase away the darkness.

And so it was that the traditions of Lussi and Lucy were combined.

> Be not afraid of darkest night!
> The stars will guide the way.
> May the Lord's Prayer give you the might
> to prevail come what may.
>
> Christian Richardt

Midwinter celebration

Celebrations were held during the dark months long before we started celebrating Christmas. Pagan sacramental feasts used to take place during the first full moon after the winter solstice. After all, there was a lot to be thankful for. For one thing, the solstice meant the days would start getting longer again. It was a celebration of the dead and of fertility that involved sacrifices to the gods and to Freyr in particular, to ensure good crops the following year. People often brought something green into their homes, such as a sprig of juniper, to signify the return of the sun and the spring – but also to protect them from the dead and from dark forces.

All these celebrations gradually combined, and traditions have lost their meaning, but we persist with them all the same. We celebrate during the dark months with lights and parties and gatherings.

But the dark forces and the perception of the dark as something negative live on – in religion and songs, in literature and language, in comic books, films, TV series and games – and in our own imaginations.

I concentrate

I look out the window. It's almost bedtime, but I'm in two minds about going to sleep. I want to sleep, because then Wednesday and daylight will come quicker, but I dread closing my eyes. I look for stars and other sky phenomena, but I can't see anything despite the big windows. Hold on, did something just dart behind that rock over there?

I have to concentrate again to make sure my imagination doesn't run wild. I know that a lot of what is swirling around in my head now is just thoughts, feelings – and that I, Sigri, am so much more than them, the consciousness that can rise above them, observe them, control them, keep them at bay. Or can I? Especially now, in the dark?

I try to think of the darkness as kind, or even light. I think about what astrophysics has taught me, about how there's no such thing as darkness, and about how I myself have written that darkness is defined as a *perceived absence* of light. There is nowhere in the universe untouched by light.

That's all well and good, but it doesn't help me much in the here and now. We should never have ordered such big windows. It feels like an eternity since I last saw another living soul.

Long Since Last We Met

what is it we do as
darkness falls and the house grows cold and it becomes even darker
and we are scared as we each busy ourselves with our own task and
we think that no one can leave us now
then we could not live in the house any more
we would have to leave because the trees hills sea everything is dark
and black when we are alone and it is long since last we met

Jon Fosse

Let it go. I drift off. Actually fall asleep. I'm surprised, even though I managed to fall asleep last night as well. I wouldn't have thought it was that easy to fall asleep while scared. Then a thump wakes me up. What in the holy hell was that? Was it the sledge outside? Was it snow? Just the wind? Or was it exactly what I'm afraid of?

I go out into the hall, fetch the axe and put it on the pillow next to me in bed. I switch on my phone, just in case. Fall asleep and wake up and fall asleep. Need to pee.

Blink and look at the axe.

DAY 3

Wednesday

Day three at the cabin, and it's so windy that I don't dare venture outside. I stay in. Declare myself weather-bound. It doesn't matter how much I want to go home now – I'm stuck here. Oh well. I make breakfast, crispbread and cod roe, and boil an egg. I think and write and read and feed logs to the stove. I look out at the storm, unable to see much else. Setting out for the station and civilisation in this weather would be insanity. Everything I could see yesterday is gone. The mountains are gone. All the rocks. All I can see is white. The wind howls and screeches, and I find myself thinking about how it's the middle of winter and wondering whether the windows will hold, or the cabin, or the chimney. What will I do if they don't? And what if the wind picks something up, a rock, for example, and hurls it through

85

the window, shattering the glass and blowing the outside in? What will I do then?

I remind myself I have warm clothes and a sleeping bag that can withstand a lot, and I thank my lucky stars that it's not dark right now. If this turns into a crisis, I can dig my way out, find another cabin and stay there until the storm dies down. I think that's allowed in a life-or-death situation. Needs must, right?

The window rattles. Shakes.

Christiane

'What if such a storm were to lift the cabin?' Christiane muses.

It is late autumn and she is all alone. A terrible storm rages outside. The men are far away on trapping business, each in a different location, on one of their last excursions before the darkness descends in earnest. It suddenly occurs to her that she should secure everything outside the cabin so that nothing is carried away by the wind. She quickly gets dressed and trots outside.

'I had never seen anything like it in all my time in Spitsbergen! The entire landscape was in turmoil. The snow swept like a tidal wave across the ground, engulfing the cabin and hanging like a cloud over the black sea. There was a deafening rumble, and high up in the air the storm boomed like a deep, drawn-out note from an organ.'

She does not have much wood, so she starts chopping some of the logs stacked against the wall of the cabin. The snow whirls up into her face and inside her anorak. She has not secured her hood properly and it soon freezes like a pipe around her head. She throws the logs through the door of the cabin. Along with the axe and the saw frame.

She continues to chop the wood inside. She tries to fire up the stove, but the flame keeps going out. The room gradually fills with smoke and she has gone through a lot of patience, paraffin and blubber by the time the stove finally lights.

It is pitch-black outside when she finally has a cup of hot coffee in her hands. She is wearing a leather gilet and leather hat, but the stove is still smoking and it is still cold in the cabin. She draws their new curtains, but her discomfort persists. The wind howls, the storm and surf roar, and the cabin is not impervious to their ire.

Days pass.

'Slowly, my hands begin to shake. [...] When pitted against an Arctic storm of this nature, every human being is reduced to a primitive individual, small and full of fear.'

Christiane does not know up from down, neither in herself nor the cabin, which is gradually snowed under. She fears that her very being might shatter. She does not have anyone to help her stay grounded. She busies herself about the cabin, as she feels this might be the only way to keep going. It is hard. She can feel the madness trying to take hold. Day after day she soldiers on, drawing on a strength that she did not know she possessed. With a kind of 'wild persistence that is renewed each day'.

'For the first time, I understand that everything takes on new meaning when one is alone against the immensity of nature rather than in a world full of interaction with other people. I understand now that in many cases it can be more difficult to preserve one's identity than one's life when faced with the elements in the Arctic.'

For nine days and nine nights, Christiane is alone. For nine days and nine nights, the storm rages without pause.

The storm in Spitsbergen

I make pancakes for lunch – quite the luxury – before shuffling outside to fill the snow bucket and giving the cabin a sweep. It doesn't take long. I'm not snowed in, the windows are still intact and the wind is passing by. Screaming and howling and whining. With a jolt, I suddenly remember another storm, a storm that was more like a hurricane. We were skiing in the north of

Svalbard in March, and the weather report was extremely good. It promised us a mild breeze and sun and a lot of laughter. There were seven of us walking with heavy sledges beneath a bluish-grey sky, a bright, white orb shining down on everything. It was the second day of our excursion, we were 300 kilometres from the nearest road, in the far north of Spitsbergen, and we were planning to walk for weeks. It was calm when we stopped for lunch on that second day, but then the wind picked up. After a while we set up camp, the temperature dropped and it wasn't powder snow any more, but heavy, wet, concrete-like snow. We did our best to keep it away from two of the tents. And we smiled. We weren't afraid, not yet. All the snow from the glacier and the whole world ended up here, but it would settle down again, it would settle down again, it had to settle down again, it needed to settle down again. We had the occasional glimpse of sky above this white inferno. It was astonishingly blue. Where was all this wind coming from? I'd always loved wind, but now? Now I wasn't so sure any more.

Evening drew in and the snow continued to fall. Hours and thoughts and focus dissolved. We abandoned one of the tents after the poles snapped, and we soon realised we wouldn't be able to save the second tent either. It was Sunday morning by this point, and we were keeping the coordinator in Longyearbyen updated by satellite phone. We considered trying to get to a cabin 10 kilometres away, but we weren't sure we still possessed the wits to manage it. We tried to dig out some ski poles sticking up out of the concrete snow, but they wouldn't budge. The skis themselves and the sledges were already buried. That was when I blacked out.

I was dragged into the remnants of one of the tents, and the wind was screaming, and someone peeled off all my wet clothes, and I remember coming round and thinking, *oh shit*. Real heroes and heroines aren't saved. They save themselves or others or die trying.

We decided to stay where we were. We started digging. We'd all spent nights out in the open during the winter, but never in conditions like this. We later learned that this valley was like a trench, funnelling the wind and increasing its speed, and theories were put forward about freezing rain and turbulence and something about the Hinlopen Strait and Sorgfjord and the storm raging on for another twenty-four hours, but we didn't know any of that out where we were. We dug to keep ourselves moving so that we wouldn't freeze. It was about half past one and we had been digging and cooling down by turns for about fourteen hours. We hadn't slept in thirty hours. The landscape was 2 metres higher and the snow was rock-hard. Then we heard the helicopter. Basically, everything worked out so well that we only warranted a couple of lines in the newspapers. Thank God for that.

A few days later I realised that any wind whatsoever made me feel nauseous. A mild breeze waltzing with the snow outside the window was enough. The severity of the situation had finally dawned on me, and my body reacted by shutting down. I felt heavy, dizzy. But still so relieved. So thankful that we'd been saved. Humbled and determined to learn something from the experience. Hindsight is a wonderful thing. What could we have done differently? Left the tent earlier? Circumnavigated unsafe and old sea ice, ice that was rising and stacking, piling up? Should we have tried to find a more detailed weather report? Or is there just some weather where even if you do everything you can, and correctly, there's still no guarantee that you will be okay?

We were in the wrong place at the wrong time, so there's probably no point agonising over it all. I'm not stupid. I know hurricanes are real. I know I'm going to die one day. And still the wind makes me feel queasy. Some people think wind can trigger the nervous system in the same way that darkness and phobias and fear can. That it's something primordial. That the alarm centre in our bodies is activated because actually, there is quite simply some weather we shouldn't be out in.

The old trappers in Svalbard knew that weatherproof clothing didn't help. That nature would always come out on top. We're not made for that kind of weather.

As experienced overwinterer Odd Ivar Ruud put it: 'A man cannot conquer all the realities of nature.'

But staying in didn't always help, either. Many people have lost their lives at sea or in miserably small cabins. Many people just disappeared. Perhaps they got lost in the wind or darkness. Wind and darkness can make seemingly easy terrain and excursions difficult, impossible or even dangerous, regardless of whether there are any crevasses, avalanche risks or unsafe patches of ice.

Where does the wind come from?

Wind is air in motion. Air that moves. John Smits, a meteorologist at the Norwegian Meteorological Institute, explains that our atmosphere strives to maintain a constant balance. It wants things to be fair, for the temperature and pressure to be the same everywhere. However, this balance is disrupted by the sun rising and setting, and by how much landscapes vary. Undeterred, the atmosphere does what it can – and one of the things it can do is move the air around. Uneven warming of the planet contributes to different temperatures, which in turn leads to different pressures and the air moving from high pressure to low pressure areas to even out the differences.

Smits says that it is somewhat windier in Norway now than

when records began in 1965, but that this is nothing compared to the increase we see in connection with temperatures and precipitation.

The danger posed by the wind depends on who you are and where you are.

'Sure, an experienced snowkiter might encounter a storm in the mountains, but the owner of a small boat who only uses it on Oslofjord a couple of days a year might just as easily get into trouble in a moderate breeze. In Eastern Norway, alarm bells start ringing when the wind gets up to 20 metres per second, which is when trees might fall and roofs and trampolines might be blown away. In Western Norway and the north, most of what isn't screwed down is already gone, so it's not usually as dangerous,' he says.

The wind is stronger by the sea, and then it encounters resistance in the form of trees, hollows and valleys that slow it down as it makes its way further inland. But when it reaches the mountains again, where the landscape is barer and there is less friction, it picks up. So-called 'exposed areas' known for being particularly windswept include, for example, protruding headlands or islands with high mountains.

Put simply, the wind is affected by what it encounters. And the higher you are in the atmosphere, the windier it gets. Different cloud formations can warn us about approaching winds.

Christiane

The men return to Gråhuken. But they have not seen the last of the storms. On one occasion, it seems to them as if there is a ring around the moon. Karl says that this portends bad weather, and sure enough, the following evening heralds the arrival of an explosive storm. There is not a lot to impede the wind in Spitsbergen's barren landscape.

The storms rage on. This does not stop Hermann, Christiane's husband, from venturing out once more. Christiane lies awake at night, wondering how anyone could possibly walk upright in such a tumult – wouldn't they simply be blown away like a splinter of wood?

'Anyone who dares venture out in such a storm is hopelessly lost! The sound of the storm and the sea is staggering. [...] It is a dark hell that howls all night long.'

The storms keep coming.

Night draws in again

Wednesday is buffeted along in Finse, the wind ravaging and sweeping the landscape. The hours drag at a completely different tempo, and I sit by one of the big windows, looking out, reading a little, trying to write. I don't feel as nauseous any more. When the wind finally dies down for a while, I start dreading the darkness, but I'm not as scared as I have been. After all, I've managed to get to sleep the other nights. Somehow. All I need to do is take the blue hour seriously and let my body relax. Not switch on any lights. And say *let it go*. I sit on the sofa and look out, as is my ritual. Crochet. The stove has died down, so I fire it up again. The cabin is much colder when it's windy. I can see my neighbour's outside light now it's quieter and starting to get darker. It's still irritating, but not as much as before. If anything should happen to the windows here, it's nice to know that there are other cabins.

What happens to our brains when it gets dark

When it gets dark, our pupils dilate to let more light in. When photoreceptors in our eyes register less light, a signal indicating that *night has fallen* is sent to our pineal gland, which is as small as half a pea and located just above our midbrain. When the brain is no longer receiving daylight signals, this gland starts secreting the hormone melatonin.

Melatonin is our darkness hormone.

The secretion of the hormone peaks between three and four o'clock in the morning. Production decreases the older we get.

Melatonin readies us to sleep by dilating the blood vessels in our skin so that our body temperature drops, among other things. This makes us feel tired and want to go to bed.

The hormone can also affect our libido – and is a very important antioxidant that protects cells from harmful mutations and helps our immune system to activate white blood cells at night.

And it is in precisely this field that revolutionary research is currently being conducted: at the start of the 2000s, it was discovered that in addition to image sensors, cones and rods in our retina, there is also a type of photoreceptor in a layer of cells we thought only contained coupled cells that were not sensitive to light.

The researchers found out that when blue light reaches these newly discovered cells, a reaction is triggered that stops the secretion of melatonin. They also discovered that it is this light that elicits the greatest response from these receptors.

This is a contemporary issue. Although incandescent bulbs and electric lights have existed for 130 years, these emit a lot more red and yellow light – calming light. Most LEDs use blue light, and unfortunately these dominate not only in street lights, outdoor lighting and tunnel lighting, but also in all the screens we surround ourselves with: in iPads, computers, mobile phones . . .

As well as having a different temperature and shorter

wavelength, blue light also has a different frequency. It flickers instead of flowing. Some people think that the temperature is the biggest problem, and others think it is the frequency.

Insects are dying and people are falling ill

Artificial light also affects insects and other animals. Everything that lives, in fact. Flowers and plants open and close depending on the light. And fall dormant in the winter. Trees, the biggest plants on Earth, shed their leaves in the autumn to conserve energy, reducing their activity through the snow and winter. But how do they know when to start growing leaves again in the spring? Well, plants and trees register the return of the light and how warm the air is before budding and growing their leaves back. Artificial light can disrupt this process. Pollination, too. Researchers have discovered that plants illuminated by street lights receive 62 per cent fewer visits from pollinating insects than those in natural darkness.

Artificial light also disrupts insect reproduction. And this is dramatic. The human population has doubled in the last forty years, and the insect population has halved. Insects don't need us, but we need them. Researchers don't think we would last more than a few months if insects were to completely die out. There are many reasons why they are disappearing, and light pollution is one of them, because these small flying creatures are drawn to light when it gets dark, which is why you should always close your windows on dark spring and autumn evenings. The main theory as to why they do this is that they think the light is the moon and fly in circles towards it. The increasing use of outside lighting means that these tiny creatures are circling their way to certain death. And even though some city insects are now in the process of changing their behaviour, studies show that hundreds of millions of insects are killed every season in big cities.

Light at sea is also problematic. Birds crossing the North Sea are fooled by illuminated oil rigs. They fly towards the artificial, floating light and exhaust themselves circling the rigs. Some of them never make it to where they were supposed to be going.

Artificial light is not only a problem for animals that fly. It makes it more difficult for predators to hunt. Frogs can be blinded for several hours by one car passing. When it is difficult to see the stars, for example in cities, some animals have trouble orientating themselves. Newly hatched sea turtles on beaches struggle to find their way back to the sea as they are supposed to, using the moonlight and stars. Dung beetles, who navigate using the Milky Way, can also end up going the wrong way. Swedish researchers worked out this form of navigation when they started studying *Scarabaeus satyrus*, a small African beetle. The female works at night, rolling small balls of dung that she uses as both a food source and somewhere for her larvae to grow. To lay them in peace, it is important that she moves these dung balls away from all the other beetles – which means it is crucial that she finds the right way and does not veer too far off course. The researchers noted that the insect even managed this at night. They also noted that she crawled up on to the dung ball and performed a dance of sorts, as if trying to work out where she was.

The experiment proved that the beetles navigate using the light. If there was no moon, they could use the stars, and even when it was overcast, the light from the Milky Way could help them find their way.

Most animals and plants also have circadian rhythms, just like us humans, meaning that they need both light and darkness in the right doses. Global warming, land development and light pollution cause problems when it comes to biological diversity. A number of studies show that night shifts and artificial light too close to bedtime can have a negative effect on our health. And this might have to do with the frequency and temperature of the light. We discovered the link between sleeplessness and depression and increased use of screens a long time ago. A detailed report from 2012 shows that there are more and bigger problems than we initially thought. There is a higher risk of morbid obesity, breast cancer, diabetes and depression in people exposed to artificial light when it is otherwise dark. It can also cause early puberty.

Orange glasses to shut out artificial light

The use of light for therapeutic purposes is old news, but the world is finally opening its eyes to the concept of dark therapy as well. They started by testing whether a person's circadian rhythm could be restored by having them stay, voluntarily, in a completely dark room for a certain amount of time. Then shift work researchers had a great idea: what about using glasses to preserve the circadian rhythm of those who have to work nights? Orange glasses can block out blue light, thereby ensuring that melatonin production doesn't stop despite all the artificial light that we are exposed to. Psychiatrist James Phelps also applied this idea to patients with bipolar disorder who experienced trouble sleeping, positing that it might make sense to trade in dark rooms for orange glasses.

At Valen Hospital, where the poet Olav H. Hauge was committed and which was also the first Norwegian hospital to be electrified, they conducted a study that validated this idea in the period 2012 to 2015. In the end, they were able to present astonishing results. Bipolar patients and people with sleep disorders that they had been trying to treat for months using medication experienced great improvement after only a week – just by regulating the light they were exposed to and wearing glasses. They found out that if their eyes were shielded from blue light from six in the evening, the manic hyperactivity disappeared and they experienced a better quality of sleep.

The Norwegian doctor who worked on this, Tone Elise Gjøtterud Henriksen, has garnered a lot of attention and been awarded several prizes for her research. She stated in an article that these glasses might help shift workers, adults with ADHD, young people who stay up playing games late into the night, those with postnatal depression and people working far into the evening who are utterly determined to get this or that damned report out of the way.

And this is important. A lot of melatonin is still prescribed in tablet form to young people who have trouble sleeping. Many hyperactive patients are still treated in brightly lit hospital rooms without sunshields on the windows.

Tone tells me more about how important melatonin is. That it synchronises the circadian rhythm of our entire body. That there are clocks in all the cells in our body – and that this hormone is like a conductor trying to ensure that all the clocks are ticking in unison by letting them know when it is night.

'But when it comes to summer and winter in Norway, how is it even possible for us to sleep during the bright, bright summer nights?' I ask her.

'Our eyes and brains are always adapting. There are also major individual differences in how sensitive we are to light. The light history of the individual is very important,' she says.

The first month of our life is important. But so are yesterday, last week and last month. This means that when there is little light in the winter, our system becomes extra-sensitive and we need more darkness to produce melatonin, whereas in the summer it becomes less sensitive and we don't need as much darkness.

That's why Tone's entire family uses orange glasses during the winter to shut out blue light, whereas there is less need for them in the summer.

'During the winter it's "put on your glasses" and "brush your teeth" every evening,' she says.

They put the glasses on two hours before bedtime.

'Darkness has become a scarce resource. The use of artificial light is increasing at an exponential rate. The iPhone was launched in 2007, and now everyone has one. Incandescent lamps were banned in 2012, so now everyone uses LEDs. It's as if everyone has very suddenly started eating really unhealthily,' she says.

She doesn't think that using orange glasses is anything more than a return to the way things were before screens and LEDs.

'In an artificially lit existence, there is relatively little difference between night and day, and this has a negative impact on us. It's unnatural and can cause trouble in our bodies.'

The body has some tasks it performs at night and others it performs during the day, and all of them are equally important. The muscles don't need to do as much at night, and the same goes for the stomach and gut. This is a time for rest, repairs and recharging. Melatonin also causes the blood vessels in our hands and feet to expand, keeping us warm. The tips of our fingers and toes are cold during the day, but when the temperature is evened out, this signals that it is night and time to rest.

So what happens if you are exposed to blue light in the middle of the night? If, for example, you wake up and check your phone, which isn't even in night mode and therefore emitting a warmer light, and scroll absently through all the latest updates from aunts and nephews and the people you follow on Instagram? Trouble, that's what.

Because as you may have realised by now, it only takes a second for the blue light from your phone to reach the receptors in your eyes, which sends a signal to the alarm centres in your brain and wakes you up properly – stopping the secretion of the darkness hormone.

'If you're lying there trying to drop off as you scroll, even if only for a few minutes, you're losing out on a huge dose of melatonin,' Tone explains.

The frequency and temperature of the blue light also stimulates the sympathetic nervous system, the same system that is activated when you are scared, so it could take a while for you to settle again.

'Are you able to say something specific and brief about how important darkness is? And how important light is – the balance between them?'

'I think we've been blind to this for much too long, but now we're starting to work it out,' she says.

Tone mentions that valuable studies have been conducted in some places. In Israel, for example, they have demonstrated that the amount of light you are exposed to at night is a contributing factor to breast cancer. The patients were asked about what street lights were like where they lived and how light their bedrooms were. It has also been proven that nurses who work at night are at greater risk of breast cancer.

Tone says there is too little research on this in psychiatry, but that darkness therapy has been very effective so far.

'We're more like flowers than we care to believe,' she says.

'Do you think the increasing number of people with depression and the high suicide rate in Norway might be linked to all of this, the fluctuating light conditions and extremely high use of artificial light during the winter?'

'I'm afraid they might be, but no one has actually conducted those specific studies. It would be prudent to look into it.'

But we do know that many people become depressed in this country and that the number of young people in this group is increasing. There have been studies demonstrating this.

'Is it okay to use these glasses without consulting your GP?'

'You have to remember that as soon as you put them on, it becomes naturally dark for your brain. That's why you shouldn't drive or engage in other risky activities while wearing them. You should start using them gradually and for no more than two hours before bed. If you can stick to that, you should be safe.'

Tone thinks it might be possible to get the glasses on prescription. And her success continues even though she is still finishing her PhD. Dark therapy with glasses is being adopted in more and more countries. And use of medication is decreasing. Glasses are being tried for more and more different types of disorders and groups of people.

She and the other researchers want to equip us with a new concept: light hygiene.

'Imagine what it would be like if everyone thought a bit more about, and was a bit more conscious of, their exposure to darkness and light. If that were the case, I think we could save a lot of resources and mitigate a lot of suffering,' she says.

'Thank you, and good luck with your important work for the benefit of humankind,' I say, immediately conscious of how pompous I sound. But I really mean it.

After all, we can but hope that all this research influences the kind of light used in both indoor and outdoor lights in the future. And at the very least that it helps raise awareness. Perhaps we'll all eventually realise that the screens, lamps and everything else we have in our homes can be adjusted and dimmed, and that they have off buttons. Then we can switch everything off and welcome both tiredness and darkness when evening draws in.

What a wonder. The human body, I mean. We know so much, yet so little. Just like with the universe – that endless space.

Storms and stars

Pitch darkness closes in on Wednesday. I know it will get light again tomorrow, and even though I'm not as afraid any more and have a better understanding of how important the darkness is, I still feel uneasy. I'm still not entirely sure how to handle it. I try to focus on breathing. Deep breath in, even deeper breath out. I lie down on the floor. Breathe. Close my eyes. When I open them again, I have to blink.

Because yes, I can see and hear the wind, the black and white and grey snowstorm enveloping everything on the ground and up to a height of 3 or 4 metres, but above that I can see an expanse of dark sky, and I can see stars. Finally.

Clear, bright stars. And the Milky Way.

The wind has swept away all the clouds, revealing the stars shining in the firmament. Shining and shining above the wind. What a sight. The windows in this cabin are new and high, almost giving me the sense of being outside. I've never seen anything like it. If I'd been outside, I'd have been standing in the middle of the snowstorm. In here, I can see far more. And much further up. I think about what Jon Fosse wrote: you can never see further than in the dark.

This is a rare sight. I completely agree with Erling Fjeldaas that the night sky needs to be preserved. That people need to wake up and see this, to realise how much unnecessary artificial light we are surrounded by – and how much harm it is doing. Parliament needs to discuss it. ASAP. There should be national parks in Norway for seeing all of this. This sight is reason enough to move here, to the mountains.

In any case, this is the best place I have to see the stars. The Milky Way. It always has been. On the rare occasions there isn't a cloud in the sky in Finse, the stars are clear and bright. I remember us all putting on our warm clothes and going outside. Dad pointing and explaining. Explaining that the stars emit their own light, that they're suns with fuel inside them, and planets and moons and comets shine because they reflect the light from the sun. Explaining that some of them are already dead. And that we look back in time when we look up because it takes time for the light to reach us. We stood in the cold and looked and looked. For Arcturus, an old star, red in colour – probably so old that it will soon die. We looked for the Big Dipper as well and drew a line from its two outermost stars to find the North Star, located about 323 light years from our sun, and which is actually three stars that have been given many names: the Pole Star; Stella Polaris; Polaris.

Using the Big Dipper and the North Star, it is also possible to find the constellation Cassiopeia on the other side of the sky. It consists of five stars in the shape of a W, two of which are the brightest in our galaxy.

The universe is the greatest mystery of our existence, and when we hide the night sky behind too much light, we also deprive ourselves of an infinite amount of knowledge. The stars aren't just the beginning, but also our continuation – the night sky has shaped our culture and our stories and will be there as long as we exist. There is comfort to be found in that.

Nicolaus Copernicus, who looked up into the heavens in

the sixteenth century, claimed that the planets orbited the sun, rather than the other way round. This discovery was so important that it is deemed the start of the scientific revolution that led to more and more discoveries, paradigms and new perceptions of the world.

The night sky gave us our first calendars, and dung beetles aren't the only creatures to have navigated using the stars – we did, too, for hundreds of years, over sea and land. The Vikings called the North Star *leiðarstjerna* (the guiding star), and used it to find their way north and home across the sea.

And telescopes keep getting better. The best now orbit the Earth as satellites, sky phenomena in their own right, giving us unique images of space as it is and has been. Our atmosphere refracts and filters the light from the universe, which is why space telescopes take the best pictures. Both of the planets in our own solar system, and of the Milky Way, which is our galaxy – a blanket of around two hundred billion stars, many of which have their own planets orbiting them. It appears as a white band of light stretching from horizon to horizon across the night sky, hence the name. What is astonishing is that this galaxy, our galaxy, is only one of many billions of galaxies with millions of black holes of various sizes, and all of this extends further than our telescopes can see. And it is always expanding. So I think it's high time we learn a bit more about the mysteries of the universe, such as those black holes. What are they? Can they be explained?

Black holes and darkness in the universe

Stars that have used up all their fuel can become black holes. Although researchers don't think there is true darkness in the universe, black holes do exist. Dead stars collapse – and contract. When the stellar mass becomes that concentrated, the gravitational force also becomes so strong that eventually not even light – which is the fastest thing in the universe, able to travel at around 300,000 kilometres a second – can escape its pull. And this is how they were named: *black* because they emit no light, *hole* because everything is pulled towards them, never to return. Everything that gets close enough is sucked in. You would be as well, if it were possible for you to get close enough. And there, close to a black hole, time and space lose the significance we have given them.

Albert Einstein was the first person to mention a black hole as a theoretical possibility. He explains gravitational force in his general theory of relativity, which has greatly helped our understanding of it. Classical physics, with Isaac Newton at the forefront, dominated before Einstein came along. This explains gravitational force as a force between point masses. Einstein knew that energy and mass are two sides of the same coin. And that energy creates gravitational force, not mass. His theory stipulates no limits on the strength of the gravitational force or the compactness of the matter.

Black holes have existed for billions of years, but our tiny human minds have only taken notice of them in the last fifty years. Paradoxically, and to my great comfort, from a great distance black holes don't look black, but light, because everything that is being pulled towards them at tremendous speed lights up.

In *Seven Brief Lessons on Physics*, Carlo Rovelli writes: 'What we see does not cease to astonish us. We realize that we are full of prejudices and that our intuitive image of the world is partial, parochial, inadequate. [. . .] The world continues to change before our eyes as we gradually see it more extensively and more clearly.' He uses this book as a platform to explain a little of everything that is so difficult to understand.

He writes that it is both naive and childish of us to believe that this corner of our entirely ordinary galaxy contains anything special, and that there are quite definitely countless other forms of astounding complexity out there in the limitless space of the universe.

Does anyone seriously live their entire life without thinking about all this?

The night sky and dark matter

But black holes are not the only darkness in the universe. According to astrophysicists, all galaxies are surrounded by a large halo with such a strong gravitational force that it deflects light and pulls the stars towards it. But it cannot be seen, and researchers do not know what it is. It is not made of the building blocks with which we are familiar, such as atoms, neutrinos or photons. They call it *dark matter* – and it makes up as much as 24 per cent of the universe. There is also *dark energy*, which makes up an even greater part of the universe, and about which we also know very little, apart from the fact that it must exist if we are to explain how the universe is always expanding.

Black holes and dark matter and energy are exceptions from the astrophysical truth that there is no darkness in space.

It is easier to explain why we perceive the night sky as black. There may be two reasons for this: one is that there isn't actually anything in that direction, nothing at all. Or it might be that what is in that direction is both far away and faint, and that our eyes are therefore not good enough to perceive this light.

Ninety-six per cent is a mystery

Research and theories about the world are always changing. Astrophysicists are always finding new moons and planets, and big unresolved problems and parallel and incompatible theories about the world abound.

Because actually, only 4 per cent of the universe consists of the ordinary matter with which we are familiar. And that's only as far as we're aware. The rest, 96 per cent, is a complete mystery. Ninety-six per cent! To me that's wild, unbelievable, sensational. Just think of all those people who dare to be so absolutely certain of everything between heaven and earth.

And we ordinary people, who have faith in God or Allah or social democracy or the good in people or love, and at the very least in what we can actually see around us, and think that we believe in science; well, perhaps we're naive. Because unfortunately researchers think that what we can see around us is also an illusion, that there isn't anything to believe in – only a very blurry image of a dense swarm of elementary processes. The wavelengths our eyes can see just happen to be so long that we're unable to differentiate the particles from each other.

Rovelli writes: 'For now, this is what we know of matter: a handful of types of elementary particles, which vibrate and fluctuate constantly between existence and non-existence and

113

swarm into space even when it seems that there is nothing there, combine together to infinity like the letters of a cosmic alphabet.'

But we do know something

For some people, and even for researchers, this knowledge, along with everything we don't know, becomes so boundless that it can become too much, particularly for just one person. But we do know something. There is one thing that scientists agree on: that our universe as we know it is the result of a big bang that happened around 13.8 billion years ago. We know that Earth is planet number three out of at least eight, perhaps ten, planets orbiting the sun in our solar system. We know that our sun will die in around five billion years, but that it will expand and consume a few planets before it does. And your light will go out long before then, because humankind is part of the eternal cycle of birth and death. Plants and planets and stars and all living things are born and grow before they dwindle and die. And between these points, during our lives, we oscillate and pulsate, between light and darkness, between slumber and activity.

Does this unsettle me? I'm not sure. Either way I suddenly feel incredibly grateful for peaceful days when nothing happens. When my phone doesn't ring. Grateful for calm skies and still, icy water. Grateful for limited vision, as well, so I can't see all the particles whizzing and whirling in everything around me, and in myself.

It would be nice to be able to see a little better, mind, because it feels late and dark now, despite the universe and the Milky Way. It's almost bedtime. I'm still looking up at the stars, just looking and looking. I've lit a candle as well. There's no one else here now. No one outside the cabin, no one in the surrounding area. I know that now. My tiredness feels better today. Like a peaceful weight in my body. It's easier to fall asleep now, getting easier and easier, sailing away, all alone.

And the axe lies next to me on a pillow.

DAY 4

Thursday

On Thursday morning, all is quiet. Overcast and strangely quiet. I eat breakfast and shuffle out into the blue, into the windswept, ice-cold landscape, minus twelve now, and there are hard, new snowdrifts everywhere – like a world's fair that no one else has seen.

I set off on my skis, see fox tracks, see grouse, see a hare. Four days have passed since I last saw another human being. I'm not sure whether I've ever spent so much time apart from other members of my own species before.

Christiane

Christiane's very first Arctic storm, of which she spends nine days alone due to the trappers' comings and goings, eventually dies down as well. She ventures outside. She sees a light bluish-pink glow in the east. She calls it a reflection of the sun, which is slowly orbiting the Earth far below her horizon. She herself stands at a loss on the shore.

'It is as if my very being is disintegrating. [...] I feel the intense loneliness around me. There is nothing like me, no one I can meet face-to-face who can confirm my existence. I feel as if I am losing the limits of my being amidst this overwhelming, powerful nature. And for the first time, I realise what a heavenly gift a fellow human being is.'

Delight in other people. Delight in a fellow human. She does not know whether the men are alive, only that they have been out in the storm, each in a different location. She hopes that they will return. She goes back to the cabin. Sees how filthy and small and dark it is. She fires up the stove, clears away the ash, collects snow, sweeps the floor – the kind of work that brings one back to reality. She wonders why the stillness of nature has left her so shaken. Perhaps because of the terrible storm that preceded it. Perhaps it is only possible to live intensely in the opposites, in the contrasts. She is starting to understand what her husband wrote when she was at home and he was trying to lure her north: 'You need to be alone to truly experience the Arctic'.

She writes that in the future people might travel to the Arctic like people in biblical times travelled into the desert to rediscover the truth.

A white winter plateau, and trying to sleep with your eyes open

I shuffle through the snow for hours. When I finally stop, I put my gloves down on a rock, sit down and listen. To this landscape, which only yesterday was a sea of howling and whining and white chaos. The sky is still white, but all is silent. Immensely silent. I feel compelled to whisper to myself to make everything seem more real. Nothing that profound; just normal things I'd say if someone were with me.

'Look at those hare droppings there, and check out that lovely snowdrift,' I whisper.

I take pictures, but you can't take a picture of silence. There is a stillness here now that is almost unnerving. Is there anywhere as silent as a white winter plateau on a windless day? And how long can anyone spend alone before they start to feel, like Christiane did, as if their very being is disintegrating? A bit longer than four days, I expect.

I don't have much water left, so I collect some ice from the lake's shoreline before retreating back into the cabin. There's more water in ice than in snow.

Back inside, I knock the snow from my boots. Then I melt the ice and boil the water for coffee. I've been out all day and I'm starving, so for dinner I make soup using meat and vegetables that I brought with me.

As it gets darker, all the clouds disappear. Twilight is blue today. Completely blue. I fire up the stove. Read and write until evening draws in. Get ready for another night, no longer as afraid as before, but still unable to sleep.

I find myself unable to close my eyes now the storm has died down and the clouds are gone. I take my duvet out to the sofa and watch the moon rising over the mountain in the east. It's big and yellow next to the mountain, but when it rises higher, setting out on its journey across the night sky, it becomes smaller and whiter, though still sizeable. It makes its way south-west before setting in the west. I watch its entire journey, for hours, through the big windows. I still can't close my eyes. I want to sleep, but it would have to be with my eyes open, because I can't stop watching.

Thursday

I

when your heart is a moon
in the evening
the rain is also there
and the story
in your body
is the mountain's
linear movement
across the sky
within

II

I can't sleep
the fatigue is
like grass clippings
in my body

Jon Fosse

Christiane

The fog releases its hold on Gråhuken in the middle of December. They have been stumbling around in endless darkness for weeks. Now, they find themselves in a world of brilliant light.

The moon is full. The world they see around them is familiar yet completely other. New.

'Our easy progress through the glittering, moonlit landscape is glorious, intoxicating.'

Christiane writes that it would be impossible for anyone in Europe to comprehend the full moon in Svalbard. It is as if the light follows them wherever they go. 'Our minds are consumed by light, and all our being draws us to the moon.'

Moonlight and the northern dawn

It's still night-time and I can't close my eyes. The snow shines silver. I go out to pee and feel like a cat, able to see everything. I'm tempted to put my skis on, to venture out into the landscape even though it's the middle of the night. The moonlight is a gift during the polar night.

I stand outside looking for the northern lights. I've seen them here before, even though Finse is technically too far south for this sky phenomenon. *Aurora borealis* is Latin for 'northern dawn'. People used to be afraid of the northern lights. When they appeared, children would be herded inside and adults would make sure to keep something made of iron on their person, to protect them from sinister forces and from an incomprehensible evil that might try to relieve them of their heads. People were also cautioned against waving white cloths in the air.

Further south, where this phenomenon was even rarer, it could be interpreted as a portent of war, foul weather and misery. The Inuit, on the other hand, are said to have seen their ancestors in the movements of the sky, in the undulating, mysterious light.

There are both northern and southern lights, so in both the Arctic and the Antarctic. Both can be referred to as polar lights. Science has taught us that the northern lights are the sun's doing. Charged particles from the sun's atmosphere collide with gaseous particles in the Earth's atmosphere between 80 and 500 kilometres above the poles. The result is energy in the form of light.

The energy level in the particles and the composition of the gas determines the colour of the northern lights.

The dominating colours that we can see with our eyes are green, red and blue. Solar activity determines how bright the northern lights are – and when they will appear. The magnetic field of the Earth and the atmosphere determine where on Earth they appear.

The area in which the northern lights appear is referred to as the *auroral oval*, a belt around 1 to 2 degrees wide in the day sector and 5 to 10 degrees wide in the night sector. The brightest and most intense northern lights can be seen within this belt, at night. You can also see the northern lights inside the oval, but these are often fainter and less colourful. Northern lights are rarely seen outside the oval.

At night, the oval is around 23 degrees from the magnetic pole. During the day, it is around 15 degrees from the magnetic pole. This means the oval is above the Norwegian counties of Troms and Finnmark during the night, but above Svalbard during the day, which explains why it is also possible to see the northern lights in the middle of the day in the far north. It also explains why the northern lights are often brighter in Northern Norway than in Svalbard. And why the daytime northern lights in Svalbard can be brighter than the night-time northern lights.

A higher degree of solar activity can nevertheless expand the oval, which explains why I've seen the northern lights in Finse – and bright colours dancing in the night sky in Svalbard.

One of the best places in the world to study the northern lights is the archipelago in the far north. There used to be an observatory in the middle of Adventdalen, just outside

Longyearbyen. However, the town and the cars driving past soon meant there was too much light pollution, so it was moved to a mountain further away.

Christiane

'Then the bright veil unfurls into the firmament. The colours ripple as if a puff of wind has set them in motion, becoming brighter and brighter as they roll across the sky. We revel in the luminous rhythm of the spheres until the veil disappears. And then we are tiny again, struggling silently and sluggishly against the storm on Earth.'

Christiane Ritter wrote a lot about the northern lights. She writes about beams of light shooting out. About how they look like luminous glass rods being thrown from on high. About how it looks as if they are falling straight down on her, getting brighter and brighter, shining pink, purple and green, furiously dancing and rotating on their own axis across the sky, drifting like rippling veils, fading and disappearing.

'All my senses have been ensnared in the swirling, spectral light in the inconceivable beauty of the Arctic night.'

DAY 5

Friday

And then morning comes, and the sun rises on my fifth day in the mountains. I haven't slept a wink. After the moon went down, the stars shone even brighter. I saw stars and satellites and shooting stars. Everything disappeared when the morning colours emerged.

Because it doesn't just get light here at this time of year, it gets red, orange and yellow, and purple and pink above the mountains. It's an explosion of colours, and I find myself thinking: why was I so afraid? These are my mountains, I know them, they've been here the whole time, and there's the snow, and here I am. Safe inside.

It's early winter now, before Christmas, but these are definitely the February colours in Svalbard. In clear weather, when the light is slowly returning. When the days and the entire polar world are blue and sunrise moves into sunset without the fiery orb showing itself. And when the first rays of sun hit the mountains and they turn pink. One such February, at bedtime, when we were talking about our day, one of my children said:

'Mummy, you're more beautiful than the mountains when they're pink.'

I cried on the inside and smiled on the outside and tucked it away in my heart. I take it out when I need it, now they're getting older and will soon be cool young people and disappear into their own worlds. I take it out now, because I miss them.

The following month, on 8 March, on International Women's Day, the sun returns to Longyearbyen, hitting the steps where the old hospital used to be. Celebrations last a whole week.

I'll soon see the sun for the first time since I arrived in Finse. I know it will peek over the mountain to the south-east at around ten o'clock. I know it will only just manage to keep itself above the mountain in the hours that follow, and I have to say, one of the best things about moving from Svalbard is this blessing: that the sun rises every morning and goes down every evening. I've thought about that and been grateful for it every single day since we moved south.

That it always gets light, and it always gets dark. We're so lucky.

Christiane

It clears up in Gråhuken on 9 January. '[...] and at about midday, for the first time, we see a faint, reddish gleam on the horizon to the south. We are overjoyed. The world might have gone up in smoke, but at least the sun still exists, and the Earth is still in its usual orbit!'

But the reddish gleam is followed by more bad weather and further days of deepest night. It has been a hard and lean winter for the trappers in Gråhuken, with little to show for their efforts, but at least there are colours due south in the sky at the end of the month. Even though the stars are still out further above their heads. 'We look at each other for the first time in daylight and are utterly appalled. We look like plants kept in a basement, pale yellow, our skin loose and wizened.'

And even though the light is returning now, it is cold. February and March are the coldest months in the far north. As far as the temperature is concerned, winter is only just setting in. All the same, the end of the month brings a festive mood. Christiane, Hermann and Karl stand on the sea ice and watch reflected light move across the mountain. Then, just *there*, they see a bright light between the peaks. Just for a moment before it continues west. The sun has returned. Spring comes to Gråhuken. The storms have subsided. And Christiane revels in the silence. In the recumbent sun hanging over the soundless landscape.

'I feel close to the very essence of nature. [...] I have some insight into the last great secret, and all human reasoning will fade into nothing before it. If only the people down on the continent could imagine the profound peace and beauty of this icy wilderness! When the sun shines and all the storms have passed!'

She writes that you can open an encyclopedia and read about the extraordinary polar world, but you cannot know the peace, clarity and lightness of a human soul under such a radiant sky. She feels at home.

And so to bed

I was really scared, but I've calmed down somewhat in the early hours of the morning. I've spent time alone now, and tried to open my eyes to the darkness – and from an entirely logical standpoint, I know how important it is. It also helps that I've written this and it's daytime and the sun will be up soon.

Now I can put the axe back where I found it and catch the train home again.

But first, I need to sleep – until tomorrow, at least.

Epilogue

CHRISTIANE: Christiane Ritter stayed in Svalbard longer than she had thought she would. She spent the entire Arctic summer there before returning to the mainland and her daughter. Her autobiography, *Eine Frau erlebt die Polarnacht* (*A Woman in the Polar Night*), was published in 1938 and became a bestseller in Europe, but wasn't translated into Norwegian until 2002. I found the book in connection with a ski trip to Gråhuken, and it really piqued my interest. The Norwegian translator, Karen Ragna Nessan, let me see all the letters she had received from Christiane. In these, she wrote that the year she spent in the far north was the happiest year of her life. In a letter dated 7 February 1993, she writes: 'The winter I spent in Gråhuken was a profound experience, not just because of the overwhelming nature in the far north, but also spiritually: the long period of darkness and the subsequent re-emergence of *the world in the light!*'

Christiane Ritter lived to the age of 104.

AND ME: I must confess I'm still a little afraid, but I look more kindly on the darkness now. And I'm still learning. I've started introducing routines at home: all screens must be switched off at least an hour before bedtime. I try to be strict, and sometimes I manage. I've bought an old alarm clock so my phone can stay switched off in the kitchen at night. And I find reasons to hope. There is hope in the German rebellion against energy-saving light bulbs, in dark sky laws and in the fight for the night sky. Hope in NASA replacing the bright blue light in a space station because the astronauts were unable to sleep. And hope in amber LEDs, a variant of this efficient light source which is still expensive, but kinder to both people and nature.

There is hope in the fact you're reading this.

Sources

BOOKS

Couper, Heather and Nigel Henbest. 1996. *Black Holes*. Dorling
    Kindersley Publishing.

Fosse, Jon. 1998. *Natta syng sine songar; Ein sommars dag* (*Night
    Sings Its Songs: A Summer's Day*). Samlaget.

Fosse, Jon. 2009. *Dikt i samling* (*Collected Poems*). Samlaget.

Heber, Sigvard. 1924. *Da Bergensbanen blev til* (*Building the Bergen
    Line*). Gyldendalske Bokhandel.

Lindmo, Anne and Helle Vaagland. 2007. *Heia Mamma!* (*Hey,
    Mama!*). Aschehoug.

Lutro, Sveinung. 2017. *Skrekkelig jul* (*Chilling Christmas*).
    Cappelen Damm.

Ritter, Christiane. 2002. *Kvinne i polarnatten* (*A Woman in the
    Polar Night*). Polar forlag. (The publisher has closed down,

so the quotes from the book have been used with permission from the Norwegian translator, Karen Ragna Nessan.)

Rovelli, Carlo. 2015. *Seven Brief Lessons on Physics*. Penguin Books.

Ruud, Odd Ivar. *Arktiske døgn (Days in the Arctic)*. Hjemmets bokforlag.

Samset, Bjørn H. 2018. *Lys (Light)*. Spartacus forlag.

Sandberg, Sigri. 2012. *Polarheltinner (Polar Heroines)*. Gyldendal.

Sverdrup-Thygeson, Anne. 2018. *Insektenes planet (Extraordinary Insects)*. Stenersens forlag.

Therkelsen, Line. 2017. *Magisk jul (Magical Christmas)*. Orage.

Visted, Kristofer. 2016. *Jul i gamle dager (Christmas in a Bygone Era)*. Spartacus forlag.

Zern, Leif. 2005. *Det lysande mørket – om Jon Fosses dramatikk (The Luminous Darkness: The Theatre of Jon Fosse)*. Samlaget.

Åmås, Knut Olav. 2004. *Mitt liv var draum – ein biografi om Olav H. Hauge (My Life Was a Dream: A Biography of Olav H. Hauge)*. Samlaget.

NEWSPAPERS AND MAGAZINES

Various articles about Terje Larsen, the Wanderer, from newspaper archive Retriever from the newspapers *Bergens Tidende*, *Ringerikes Blad*, *VG*, *NTB*, *Dagbladet*, *Aftenposten* and *Bergensavisen* during the period 2001–18.

About fear of the dark: *Fjell og Vidde*, December 2014.

My account of the storm in Spitsbergen is based on a text originally printed in *Utemagasinet* in 2011.

Sources

ENLIGHTENING CONVERSATIONS AND INTERVIEWS WITH:
Asle Hoffart, professor of psychology
Erling Fjeldaas, lawyer
Janne Grønli, professor of psychology, sleep specialist
Jon Fosse, writer
John Smits, meteorologist
Petter Bøckman, zoologist
Svein Jonny Albrigtsen, miner
Tone Elise Gjøtterud Henriksen, doctor
Vegard Lundby Rekaa, astrophysicist

PUBLISHED THESES
Fjeldaas, Erling (2017) *Regulering av lysforurensning i norsk rett* (*Regulation of Light Pollution in Norwegian Law*) (master's thesis). University of Oslo.

ARTICLES ONLINE
Aiken, Chris (2018) Smartphones, Evening Light, and Childhood Bipolar Disorder. *Psychiatric Times*, 31 August. Available at www.psychiatrictimes.com
Austgulen, Rigmor (2008) Olav H. Hauge – tåler helter dagens lys (Olav H. Hauge: Can Heroes Tolerate the Light of Day?). *Tidsskrift for Den norske legeforening*, 18 December (issue 24). Available at www.tidsskriftet.no
Avner, Terje (2015) Universets sorte hull sluker alt på sin vei

(The Black Holes of the Universe Devour Everything in Their Path). *Aftenposten*, 24 March. Available at www.aftenposten.no

Berge, Torkil (2015) Hva er depresjon (What Is Depression?). *Norsk psykologforening*, 4 December (updated 16 April 2018). Available at www.psykologforeningen.no

Bjørnstad, Lasse (2015) Lyset fra skjermen forstyrrer søvn og gjør deg trøtt om morgenen (Light from Screens Disturbs Sleep and Leaves You Tired in the Mornings). *Forskning.no*, 22 January. Available at www.forskning.no

Boyle, Rebecca (2018) Kunstig lys tar over kloden (Artificial Light Is Taking Over the World). *Harvest*, 27 August. Available at www.harvestmagazine.no

Brekke, Asgeir (2005) Det farlige nordlyset (The Dangerous Northern Lights). *Nordlys*, 23 September. Available at www.nordlys.no

Børresen, Anne Kristine (2014) Geologer i felt (Geologists in the Field). *Geo365*, 4 July. Available at www.geo365.no

Dagslys (Daylight), on *Wikipedia*. Available at www.wikipedia.org

Dvergsdal, Arne (2000) Fra sykdom til mesterskap (From Illness to Championship). *Dagbladet*, 28 August. Available at www.dagbladet.no

Dæhlen, Marte (2018) Dårlig søvn er dyrt for samfunnet (Sleep Problems Are Expensive for Society). *Forskning.no*, 11 June. Available at www.forskning.no

Elstad, Hallgeir (2017) Frå Lussi til Lucia (From Lussi to Lucy).

Sources

The Faculty of Theology, University of Oslo, 13 December. Available at www.uio.no

Fjeldaas, Erling (2018) Stjernene som forsvinner (The Disappearing Stars). *Dagbladet*, 2 October. Available at www.dagbladet.no

Fobier.net (year unknown) *Fakta om fobier* (*Facts about Phobias*). Available at www.fobier.net

Fonna Hospital Trust (2017) Oransje briller gir betring til maniske pasientar (Orange Glasses Help Bipolar Patients). *Fonna Hospital Trust*, 15 June (updated 12 November 2018). Available at www.helse-fonna.no

Fyllingsnes, Ottar (2004) Olav H. Hauge: Brende Diktmanus (Olav H. Hauge: Burnt Poetry). *Dag og Tid*, 21 August. Available at www.dagogtid.no

Graven, Andreas R. (2013) Søvntyv fram i lyset (Sleep Thief Comes to Light). *Forskning.no*, 23 May. Available at www.forskning.no

Graven, Andreas R. (2013) Ungdom trenger mer søvn, men sover mindre (Young People Need More Sleep, but Are Sleeping Less). *Forskning.no*, 2 May. Available at www.forskning.no

Grønli, Janne (2014) Godt om søvn (On Sleep). *Tidsskrift for Den norske legeforening*, 25 March (issue 6). Available at www.tidsskriftet.no

Grønli, Janne, et al. (2009) Basale søvnmekanismer (Basic Sleep Mechanisms). *Tidsskrift for Den norske legeforening*, 10 September (issue 17). Available at www.tidsskriftet.no

Hammerstrøm, Maria (2018) Lysforurensning (Light Pollution), in *Store norske leksikon*. Available at www.snl.no

Haugan, Idun (2013) Mørketidsmedisin (Polar Night Medication). *Forskning.no*, 11 January. Available at www.forskning.no

Henriksen, Tone E. G. et al. (2017) Søvnproblemet kan være et lysproblem (Our Sleep Problem Might Be a Light Problem). *Aftenposten*, 18 December. Available at www.aftenposten.no

Hildebrandt, Sybille (2009) Slik virker søvn (How Sleep Works). *Forskning.no*, 19 March. Available at www.forskning.no

Hoffmann, Thomas (2009) REM-søvn løser problemene (REM Sleep Solves the Problems). *Forskning.no*, 27 June. Available at www.forskning.no

Illustrert vitenskap (2009) Hva er lysforurensning (What Is Light Pollution?). *Illustrert vitenskap*, 1 September. Available at www.illvit.no

Jakobsen, Siw Ellen (2018) Etter én eneste natt uten søvn begynner kroppen å lagre fett (The Body Starts Storing Fat after Only One Sleepless Night). *Forskning.no*, 31 August. Available at www.forskning.no

Kjensli, Bjørnar (2013) Gjødselbille navigerer etter stjernene (Dung Beetles Navigate Using the Stars). *Forskning.no*, 28 January. Available at www.forskning.no

Kristoffersen, Martin Jacob (2017) Kunstig lys kan true pollineringen (Artificial Light May Threaten Pollination). *Nationen*, 16 August. Available at www.nationen.no

Kvittingen, Ida (2014) Derfor husker noen oftere drømmer (Why

Some People Remember Their Dreams More Often).
Forskning.no, 20 February. Available at www.forskning.no

Lauritsen, Eivind Nicolai (2017) Behandling mot søvnløshet førte til færre psykiske plager (Treatment for Sleeplessness Led to Fewer Psychological Issues). *Forskning.no*, 12 September. Available at www.forskning.no

Lussi, on *Wikipedia*. Available at www.wikipedia.org

Lysvåg, Erlend Christian (2015) Mørkets øy (The Isle of Darkness). *Harvest*, 26 March. Available at www.harvestmagazine.no

Mareritt (Nightmare), on *Wikipedia*. Available at www. wikipedia.org

Melatonin, on *Wikipedia*. Available at www.wikipedia.org

Midtvinterdagen (The Winter Solstice), on *Wikipedia*. Available at www.wikipedia.org

Milde, Svein Harald (2014) Mentale bilder gir fysiske forandringer (Mental Images Result in Physical Changes). Department of Psychology, University of Oslo, 24 January. Available at www.sv.uio.no

Mortensen, Silas (2010) Spør en forsker: Hva er mareritt, og hvorfor får vi dem? (Ask a Researcher: What Is a Nightmare and Why Do We Have Them?) *Forskning.no*, 9 October. Available at www.forskning.no

Nightmare. (2019). In: *Lexico*. [online] Available at: www.lexico. com/en/definition/nightmare [Accessed 27 July 2019]

Nilsen, Lisbeth (2012) Mer bipolar sykdom hos forskere og forfattere (More Bipolar Disorder among Researchers and

Writers). *Dagens medisin*, 17 October. Available at www.
dagensmedisin.no

Nordstjernen (Polaris), on *Wikipedia*. Available at www.
wikipedia.org

Norwegian Council for Mental Health (year unknown) Depresjon
(Depression). Norwegian Council for Mental Health.
Available at www.psykiskhelse.no

Norwegian Health Informatics (2018) *Diagnostikk av depresjon*
(*Diagnosing Depression*), 27 March. Available at
www.nhi.no

Norwegian Health Informatics (2017) *Hva er søvn?* (*What Is
Sleep?*), 4 April. Available at www.nhi.no

Norwegian Institute for Nature Research (2015) Lysforurensing
påvirker alt fra encellede dyr til mennesker (Light Pollution
Affects Everything from Unicellular Organisms to
Humans). *Norwegian Institute for Nature Research* (*NINA*),
13 February. Available at www.nina.no

Norwegian Water Resources and Energy Directorate (2018)
*Kraftåret 2017: Rekordhøyt strømforbruk og høye priser til
tross for vått og varmt år* (*The Year in Power 2017: Record-
breaking Electricity Consumption and High Prices Despite
Warm, Wet Year*), 22 January. Available at www.nve.no

Oljelampe (Oil lamp), on *Wikipedia*. Available at www.
wikipedia.org

Rosvold, Knut A. (2018) Elektrisk lys (Electric light), in *Store
norske leksikon*. Available at www.snl.no

Sources

Strand, Nina (2005) Olav H. Hauge og Valen sjukehus (Olav
H. Hauge and Valen Hospital). *Tidsskrift for Norsk
psykologforening*, 1 January (Vol. 42, number 1). Available at
www.psykologtidsskriftet.no

Stranden, Anne Lise (2018) Svenske ungdommer får mer
angstdempende medisiner (Young Swedes Take More Anti-
anxiety Drugs). *Forskning.no*, 8 August. Available at www.
forskning.no

Ulfrstad, Lars-Marius (2004) Stjernehimmelen som forsvinner
(The Disappearing Starry Sky). *Aftenposten*, 2 April.
Available at www.aftenposten.no

Valmot, Odd R. (2012) Slik virker lyset på kropp og sinn (How
Light Affects Your Mind and Body). *Teknisk Ukeblad*, 11
February. Available from www.tu.no

Valmot, Odd R. (2018) Snart 150 år med strøm i Norge: Her er
elektrisitetens historie (Almost 150 Years of Electricity in
Norway: the History of Electricity). *Teknisk Ukeblad*, 11
February. Available from www.tu.no

Zevs (Zeus), on *Wikipedia*. Available at www.wikipedia.org

Various articles from www.darksky.org
Video with Tone Henriksen: www.vimeo.com/170022873

Poems

p. 27: Natt (*Night*) (excerpt), Sonja Nyegaard, from *Mørket er et mirakel*, Kolon 2018.

p. 38: Vintermorgon (*Winter Morning*), Olav H. Hauge, from *Dropar i Austavind*, Noregs Boklag 1966.

p. 64: I eit mjukt mørker (*In a Kind Darkness*), Jon Fosse, from *Hundens bevegelsar*, Samlaget 2009.

p. 66: Excerpts from the play *Ein sommars dag* (*A Summer's Day*), Jon Fosse, Samlaget 1998.

p. 80: First verse of 'Allting Freidig' by Christian Richardt, Norwegian Missionary Society, et al. *Sangboken*, A. S. Lunde & Co. forlag 1955.

p. 83: Så lenge sidan dei andre (*Long Since Last We Met*), Jon Fosse, from *Nye dikt*, Samlaget 2009.

p. 121: *I and II*, Jon Fosse, from *Hundens bevegelsar*, Samlaget, 2009.

Acknowledgements

I would like to express my profound gratitude to everyone who has shared their knowledge, and to those who have let me ramble on about it.

I would also like to thank my children, who are always ready for a good story, Mum and Dad, who took me to Finse, and Steinar, for hanging in there and propping me up.

This translation has been published with the financial support of NORLA.